W. Turner

Oxford

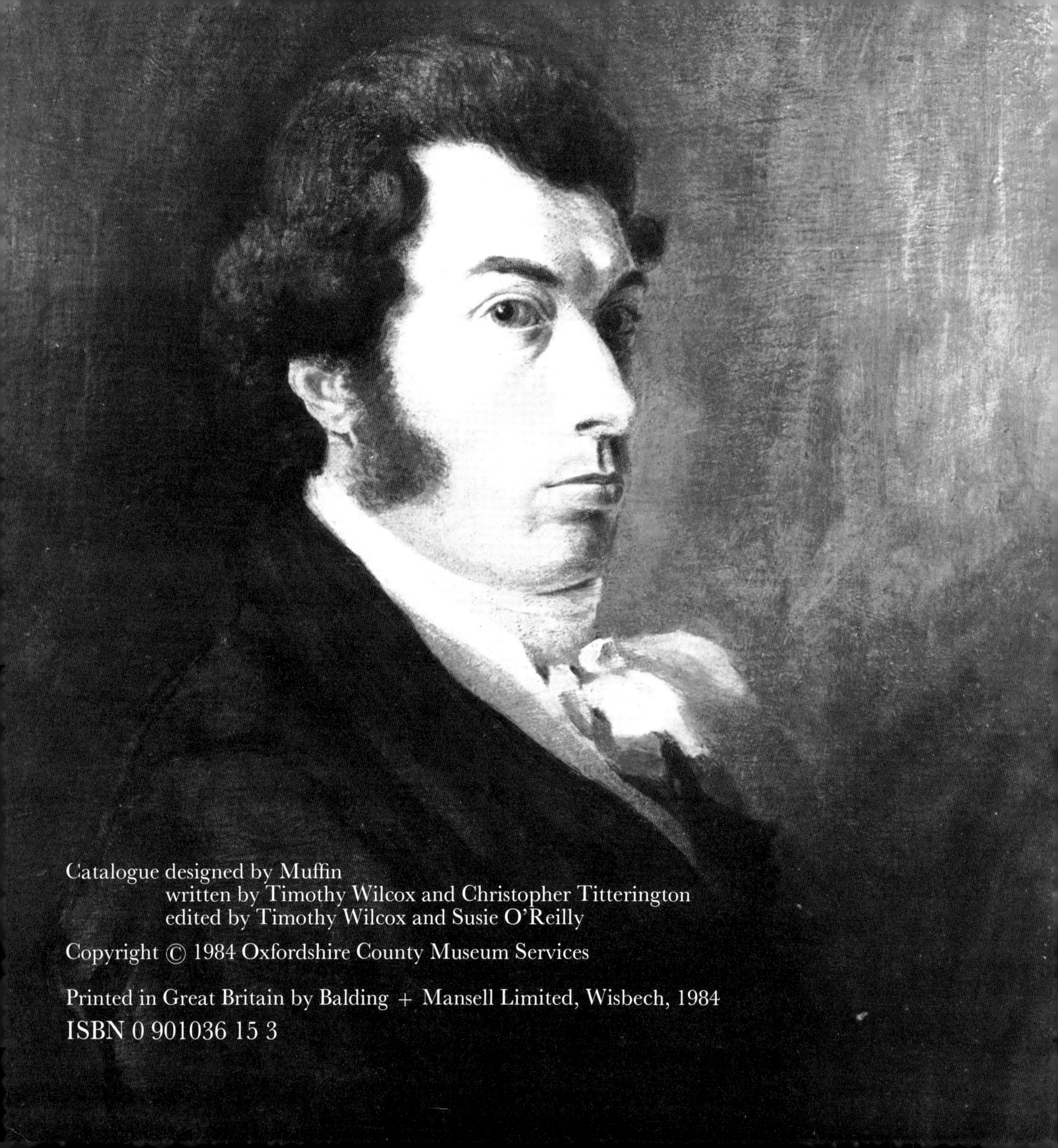

Catalogue designed by Muffin
written by Timothy Wilcox and Christopher Titterington
edited by Timothy Wilcox and Susie O'Reilly

Printed in Great Britain by Balding + Mansell Limited, Wisbech, 1984
ISBN 0 901036 15 3

William Turner of Oxford (1789–1862)

A catalogue of a touring exhibition held at:

Oxfordshire County Museum, Woodstock
9 September–28 October 1984
The Bankside Gallery, London SE1
6 November–2 December 1984
The Museum and Art Gallery, Bolton
15 December 1984–19 January 1985

SUBSIDISED BY THE Arts Council OF GREAT BRITAIN

supported by
The Marc Fitch Fund
The Paul Mellon Centre for Studies in British Art

BANKSIDE GALLERY

DINERS CLUB INTERNATIONAL

Preface

The city of Oxford has attracted the attention of a great many distinguished artists, and there have been many who, at one time or another, have lived in the County. None, however, was as closely associated with the city and its surrounding countryside as William Turner, who justly deserves his epithet "of Oxford". His allegiance to the city was evident as early as around 1810 when he began to be referred to as Turner "of Oxford" to distinguish him from the already well-established J. M. W. Turner (1775-1851). Although well-known in Oxford in his day, his death in 1862 passed unnoticed by the local press. It was not until 1895 that Dr Woods, President of Trinity College, and the Rev. H.W. Yule, Rector of Shipton-on-Cherwell, collaborated in the organisation of a memorial exhibition, which was held in the University Galleries (now known as the Ashmolean Museum). The catalogue included 179 items, all drawn from local collections. Since that exhibition there has been no other devoted solely to Turner of Oxford.

It is fitting that the Oxfordshire County Museum Services should mount this exhibition dedicated to an artist who drew so much of his inspiration from the varied landscape of the county. Fitting, too, in one sense, that the venue should be Woodstock rather than Oxford. Turner's first and greatest love was the countryside, not the town, and though he lived for 30 years in St John Street, not two hundred yards from the Ashmolean, his spiritual home was in Shipton-on-Cherwell, just two miles from Woodstock.

Turner is much more than a "local artist". This is reflected in the exhibition, which not only presents the fruit of research into Turner himself but also documents the extent of his involvement with the advanced artistic thinkers of his day. Turner emerges as an original voice, not only in his earliest years, but throughout a long and active career.

It has only been possible to bring together such a representative showing of Turner's work through the generosity of the many owners who have lent to the exhibition. Much of Turner's work remains in private hands, and to those collectors who have been prepared to endure a blank space on their walls for several months, I should like to express most sincere thanks; their contribution to the exhibition is inestimable. I am also very pleased to acknowledge with gratitude the interest in the project shown by Michael Spender of the Royal Society of Painters in Watercolours, and David Morris of Bolton Museum and Art Gallery, which enabled the exhibition to reach a much wider public. That the project has grown to its present scale is due entirely to the generosity of our sponsors, The Arts Council of Great Britain, The Marc Fitch Fund, The Bankside Gallery, London, The Paul Mellon Centre for Studies in British Art, and the Diners Club International: I am grateful to all of them for their support, particularly in making possible the publication of this catalogue.

The exhibition has been organised by Susie O'Reilly supported by many members of the County Museum Services staff. The research and the writing of the catalogue are the work of Christopher Titterington and Timothy Wilcox. All deserve a special word of thanks for the energy and enthusiasm they have brought to this lengthy task.

James A. Bateman

Director, Oxfordshire County Museum Services

Contents

Cover illustration: Boating on the Isis, Cat.49
Frontispiece: Self Portrait, 1824, Cat.43

Introduction

The Art of William Turner: Landscape and the Historical Imagination

1. Turner and the Watercolour Society

Born in 1789, William Turner belongs to the same generation as some of the greatest masters of English watercolour. He was slightly younger than Cotman, Cox and DeWint (born 1782, 1783 and 1784 respectively), but came to prominence, like them, in the first decade of the nineteenth century. The year 1805 saw the foundation of the Society of Painters in Watercolours, the first body dedicated to the promotion of what, till then, had been regarded as a distinctly second-class medium and the group of artists it gathered together rejoiced in their newly discovered sense of identity.[1] The confidence engendered in watercolour painting as a serious means of expression, and the commitment of the Society to create a market for its work, laid the foundation for the enormous nineteenth-century boom in watercolour.

The inferior position of watercolour in the eighteenth century was based partly on its limited technical development, and partly on its traditional association with topography and landscape. Within the established taste for morally elevating historical or literary subjects, landscape itself was at best an adjunct to the high purpose of art. Yet even as these attitudes were being codified by Reynolds in his *Discourses* to the students of the Royal Academy (delivered 1769–1790), there was a widespread and growing appreciation of Nature as a source of moral values. Burke's step of identifying the Sublime as an independent aesthetic category was significant, as the source of the emotions of sublimity were often the wilder landscape features and natural phenomena; mountains, waterfalls, wide open spaces or storms (*Philosophical Enquiry into the Origin of our ideas of the Sublime and Beautiful*, 1757).

The means whereby various types of scenery achieved their maximum effect in painting became a dominant preoccupation at the end of the eighteenth century in the cult of the Picturesque. The new doctrine, with its ability to accommodate all types of scenery and architecture and any amount of incidental detail as appropriate subjects for painting, did much to establish the acceptance of watercolour, which, by virtue of its relative informality and alliance with the lower branches of art, appeared eminently suited to its aims. In this favourable climate, watercolour painting made great advances, most outstandingly in the watercolour landscapes exhibited by J.M.W. Turner during the 1790s, which greatly extended the technical and expressive range of the medium and fully established its pretensions to rival anything produced in oils.

The members of the newly founded Watercolour Society (as it will be referred to from now on) pledged themselves to exhibit only as a united group and no longer at the Royal Academy. Freed from their role in the supporting cast, they had a collective incentive to show off to the best advantage what they believed, and demonstrated, to be the fullest potential of watercolour as a vehicle for art of the highest and most serious kind. Along with John Varley

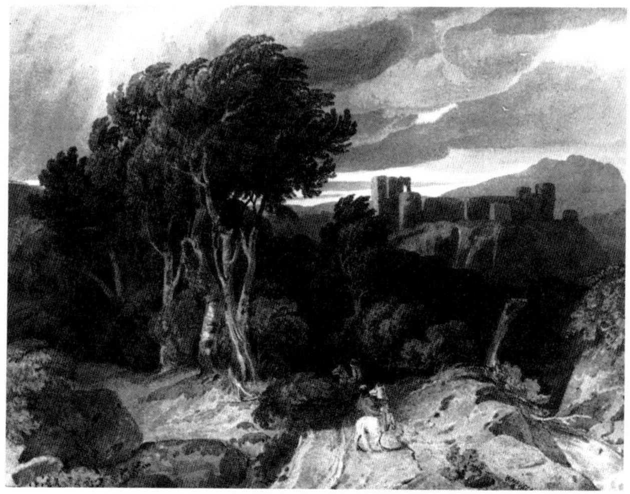

Fig. 1 William Havell (1782–1857). *Stormy Twilight.* Exhibited 1808. Photograph courtesy Christie's

(1778–1842), the most widely experienced landscape painter in the Society was William Havell (1782–1857). The critic John Landseer, did not hesitate to liken Havell's *Stormy Twilight* (1808, fig.1) to the acknowledged exemplar of serious landscape, Titian's *St Peter Martyr*, with which it "might almost vie . . . for loftiness of conception" (*Review of Publications in Art*, June 1808, p.190).

It is within the context of these years, marked by the confidence the watercolourists displayed, that William Turner's youthful work must be seen in order for its full implications to emerge. His *Whichwood Forest* (Cat.14), exhibited in 1809, is a summation of the movements of this decade. A complex work, having few rivals among the output of his fellow watercolourists, it is the first magnificent flowering of those seeds from which the whole of his art was to grow. Its outstanding qualities may seem to lend credence to the common belief that he burnt himself out at an early age, retired to the humdrum existence of a provincial drawing-master, and had said all he had to say as an artist.[2] He is, in fact, an example, very rare among nineteenth-century watercolourists, of a man who retained his youthful ardour and sense of purpose throughout his career. The range of his subject-matter is vast, but always displays a single-minded dedication to landscape, and to the creation of imposing, carefully articulated artistic statements. The early drawing of *Cornmarket* (see Cat.20) demonstrates what an efficient draughtsman Turner could be, but this was a side of his talent that he never drew attention to, or chose to develop; he never exhibited an urban scene, and country houses feature only very occasionally among 455 exhibits spread over 55 years at the Watercolour Society. Although he took to making drawings of Oxford buildings, particularly in later life when prompted by a sense of nostalgia for the passing of many of the more picturesque corners of the city, they are for the most part drab and joyless productions. Turner was not tempted either to emulate Society colleagues like Copley Fielding whose average submission to the annual exhibition was over forty works; the many smaller watercolours were easier to sell, but encouraged an empty facility of technique, and an inevitable monotony of subject, which was regretted by all commentators. Turner's commitment was to large-scale compositions which would do justice to the breadth of his conception of the natural world.

2. The landscape of association

The potential of a landscape to be both naturalistically and topographically specific and at the same time symbolic becomes the strongest undercurrent in the landscape of the nineteenth century; it is the thread that unites J.M.W. Turner and the Pre-Raphaelites (superficially dissimilar to almost everyone but Ruskin), and a host of lesser artists, William Turner among them. Within the concerns of the Picturesque, the writer who did most to increase the range of reference of the painted landscape was Archibald Alison. His *Essay on the Nature and Principles of Taste* (1790) extends the contribution made by Uvedale Price to the theory of the Picturesque. For Price (*Essays on the Picturesque*, 1784), the objects in the repertoire of the Picturesque, ivy-clad ruins, dilapidated cottages, old mis-shapen trees, achieved their distinctive value by virtue of their roughness and irregularity, qualities which inspired an appreciation of the processes of change effected by time. Alison, on the other hand, emphasised not the qualities of objects themselves but their capacity to arouse associations as the basis of aesthetic appreciation and the attibution of value. He demonstrates the strength of the theory from a number of sources. One passage, from Thompson's *Spring*, described by Alison as "one of the most picturesque circumstances ever imagined by a poet" is of direct relevance to Turner, as is Alison's commentary, which follows the quotation.

"Lead me to the mountain brow
Where sits the shepherd on the grassy turf,
Inhaling, healthful, the descending sun.
Around him feeds his many bleating flock
Of various cadence, and his sportive lambs
Their frolics play; and now the sprightly race
Invites them forth, when swift the signal given
They start away, and sweep the mossy mound
That runs around the hill, the rampart once
Of iron war, in ancient barbarous times."

Spring

"The scene is undoubtedly beautiful in itself without the addition of the last circumstance; yet how much more beautiful does it become by the new order of thought which this circumstance awakens in the mind, and which contrasting the remembrance of ancient warfare and turbulent times, with the serenity and repose of the modern scene, agitates the imagination with a variety of indistinct conceptions, which otherwise could never have arisen in it?"[3]

Much of William Turner's most characteristic work is directly illustrative of such a passage, in which the raw material of Thompson's description is taken up and expanded in the imagination, albeit in a "variety of indistinct conceptions". The analogies between Turner's work and Alison are so close that he had presumably read Alison for himself. He could have first come into contact with the theory through Varley, who, in a passage of his *Treatise on the Principles of Landscape* (c.1816) brings together the two currents of truth to nature and the wider power of association in a way axiomatic for Turner:
"A Painter must rest his pretentions to fame on an early and natural perception of the beauty of classification, and in the unity of subject . . . this faculty, so rare, and so difficult of acquirement . . . owes its power to its concealment under the garb of simple and faithful imitation of nature, each object and its accompaniments answering to the ideas instantly raised by the mention of such scenes as those in which they occur, but surpassing them by the greater perfection of those associations which rendered those ideas estimable."[14]
The ideas of "the unity of subject" and of "simple and faithful imitation of nature" as the essential foundations for the presentation of wider issues are precisely those elements which most distinguish Turner's work.

The changing face of the landscape in the wake of the industrial revolution and the introduction of modern farming methods is a theme Turner refers to again and again, if often only obliquely or by inference. In this, he employs the notion of the associational landscape and its basis in the layers of meaning present in any given scene to great effect and the sort of historical association so much

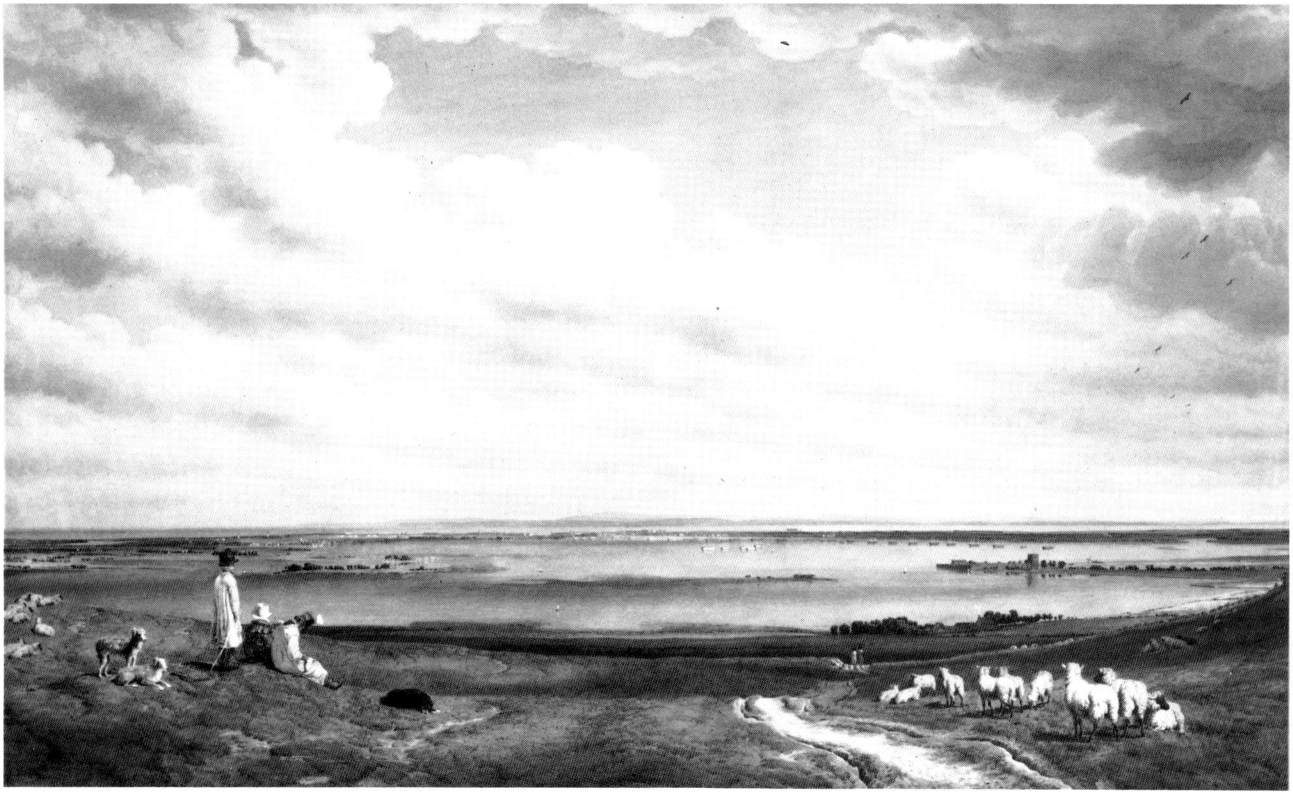

Cat.59 Portsmouth Harbour from Portsdown Hill

praised by Alison in the quotation from Thompson is common in his work. Turner is drawn repeatedly to those features in the landscape which evoke the distant past. Stonehenge is one obvious example; the belief that it was built for Druidic ritual relates the subject closely to the representations of the Druid's burial ground on Loch Maree (SPW 1842 (96), 1848 (189)). Stone circles were believed to have had a similar function; the Oxfordshire Rollright Stones appeared very early in his work (SPW 1809 (268)), while the Nine Maidens in Cornwall show the abiding fascination of a similar subject perhaps forty years later. Long barrows are not omitted from the archaeological gamut; one of Turner's exhibited works depicted the tumuli on Bow Hill, on the South Downs, and although they are not visible in all of his paintings of the spot, the name alone is surely enough to conjure up the full extent of the historical presence (see Cat.68 and 78). Copley Fielding's near-contemporary views of a similar landscape further east along the Downs have the same spaciousness, but lack the variety and contrast built into Turner's work, which help the imagination to focus more precisely on the character of the scene (see fig.2).

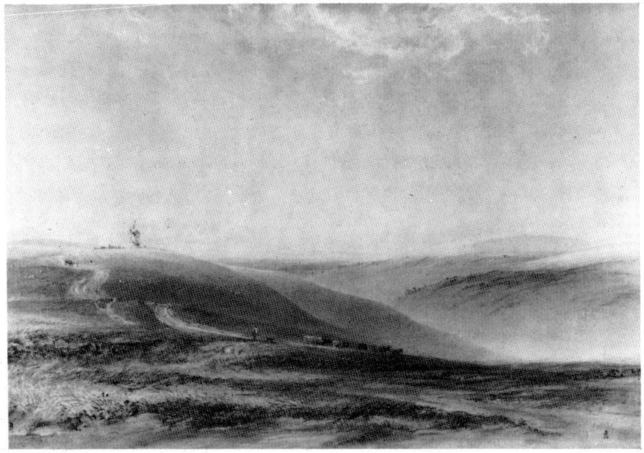

Fig. 2 Anthony Vandyke Copley Fielding (1787–1855). *A Scene on the South Downs near Rottingdean.* Dated 1849. Watercolour. Victoria and Albert Museum, Ellison Bequest

The period of early settlement is evoked not only through its more conspicuous vestiges. In one imaginative work, based on an early Oxford Prize Poem of 1791, *The Aboriginal Britons*, by George Richards (1767–1837, SPW 1843 (260); a re-issue of the poem was published in 1839), Turner depicted a landscape of "shadowy forests", "rich fruitful plains" and "majestic rivers". The idea of a landscape before cultivation, yielding its riches without the benefits of forestry, enclosure and the building of the canal systems, had a potency which was irresistible to Turner. With John Clare, the open landscape was to him equated with the idea of personal freedom.[5]

However much the neolithic monuments bore in weight of association, there were features in the present Oxfordshire landscape in which this spirit of untameable nature seemed still to survive, and Turner made them the subject of a number of major early works; Otmoor in 1808 and Wychwood Forest in 1809. His response to Wychwood seems to accord with that of the Rev. William Gilpin, first arbiter of the Picturesque, for whom the forest is an emblem of the very themes just discussed. "The forest disdains all human culture. On it the hand of nature only is impressed. The forest, like other beautiful scenes, *pleases the eye*; but its great effect is to *rouse the imagination*.[6] For all the importance of this idea, Wychwood was more than just a stimulus to the imagination; the forest was under threat of enclosure. Possibly through his uncle, a gentleman farmer at Shipton-on-Cherwell, Turner might have heard of Arthur Young's *General View of the Agriculture of Oxfordshire*, first published in 1807, where the enclosure of Wychwood was urgently recommended. The topicality of the image introduces a new element of specificity to the landscape of association.

The contemporary issues raised by Wychwood may have escaped the London audience in 1809, as may the significance of the Otmoor pictures exhibited around that date. Otmoor was well known in Oxfordshire as an area of low-lying, marshy land unfit for serious cultivation which had however offered a meagre living as common land to the inhabitants of the "Seven Towns" scattered round its lip. Prone to frequent flooding, the land itself seemed to resist attempts to enclose it and make it profitable. There was also more organised resistance: the first Bill of Enclosure, brought in 1788, was defeated in Parliament, thanks to local pressure, and a second not passed until 1815. Resentment of the move eventually exploded in 1830, with gangs of men breaking down the new fences and ditches. As about sixty of the offenders were being conveyed to Oxford jail, they came into St Giles at the height of its autumn fair. Their military escort was overcome by the crowd, and the men freed. These, the so-called "Otmoor riots", were widely reported in the London press, and the injustice of the way the enclosure had been conducted was widely condemned. Such cases, said *The Times* "directly [illustrate] the expediency, nay, necessity of some description of 'reform'."[7] With this background, Turner's gesture of sending to the London exhibition of 1831 a painting of *Otmoor, Oxfordshire – as it occasionally appeared previous to the Enclosure*, was highly provocative. The painting is now lost, but must surely have represented, along with so many of Turner's works, the attraction of the landscape in its unspoilt, open state.

The works so far discussed address major issues affecting the countryside in general. In his many paintings of the River Cherwell, the special associations of the subject are more exclusively personal. The river appears among Turner's first exhibited works in 1808, but in 1837 begins a series of works showing the river spread with water-lilies which for their quiet intensity gained the painter a certain celebrity. The decision to exhibit the Otmoor picture in 1831 implies a resistance to change on Turner's part which could at times be militant. The theme of the Cherwell pictures is the same, but the mood is elegiac. The Oxford Canal, built between about 1769 and 1776, runs alongside the Cherwell for over 20 miles between Thrupp and Banbury. For a small stretch, of a little over a mile, the canal builders took over the river, deepening the channel, and leaving a network of streams and backwaters cut off from the main stream. This took place precisely at Shipton. Turner's Cherwell is the "lost world", overgrown with willows, rushes and lilies, not the symbol of the modern, industrialised landscape. Although the full implications of the scene could not be known to every observer, its atmosphere was eloquent, prompting one reviewer in 1857 to mention "William Turner's formal but deeply-felt views of Scottish Lakes and midland streams, with their floating lilies, which, belonging as they do to the past, still speak of a sweet and profound spirit in the painter".[8]

The Scottish Lochs provided Turner with the last variation in his exploration of the associative landscape. We have seen already his predilection for the land in a state before modern cultivation, but those images all contain an element of contrast, the sense of the "now-and-then". The attraction of the Highlands was in preserving, in certain places, a landscape which appeared genuinely immaculate, free of any association whatsoever. The most compelling of such places was Loch Coruisk. Despite the influence of Walter Scott, whose imaginative response to the place in the *Lord of the Isles* was so compelling that few subsequent visitors could escape its thrall, its physical integrity remained inviolable and it served for many artists as the epitome of the landscape immune to human activity (Cat.61 and 81).

3. Truth to Nature

It is not only through the associative power of specific locations that Turner sets out his image of the landscape. His master John Varley, had a profound and lasting influence on Turner and it is in his work, more than that of any of his other pupils, that the conflicting strands of Varley's personality are most fully developed. Varley was the natural heir of Girtin in the vanguard of the watercolour school and already the leading teacher in London by about 1805; it was to him that the cream of the aspiring watercolourists turned, especially the landscape painters, Cox, DeWint and Copley Fielding. Above all, he encouraged his pupils to study from nature, and develop that truthfulness in colour and natural effect which had been a hallmark of Girtin's work. Following Varley's lead, the oil sketches made in the open-air by Cox and John Linnell, for example, mark a new directness and responsiveness of approach to nature.[9] Much of Varley's later method, however, consisted of the opposite: the deduction from the initial experience of nature of fixed laws, which would guarantee the visual orderliness and staisfaction of a painting, a method enshrined in his *Treatise on the Principles of Landscape* (c.1816), set down in a language whose categorical style leaves apparently little room for improvisation. To Varley, landscape sketching was a source of raw material, but not an end in itself; if it served to make the finished works more convincing, then this was an advantage insofar as the landscape might then exercise a more profound effect on the imagination. In Turner's work, however, the general and the specific are held in perpetual tension.

As a counterbalance to their study of nature, a number of the advanced watercolourists formed themselves into small groups, meeting together to produce washed drawings usually based on a literary text, through which they could give freer rein to fantasy and the imagination.[10] The first of these "Sketching Societies" was formed by Girtin in 1799; following his death in 1802, a group met, centred around Cotman, which included Varley, Havell and Joshua Cristall, all of whom became founder members of the Watercolour Society. These lamplit meetings were not incompatible with their avid study of nature in the open air; indeed, the best work is distinguished by a sensitive recollection of these endeavours. What is more, the exhibited work of Varley and Havell, the two men most active in both camps, displays a remarkable cross-fertilisation, resulting in large-scale watercolours at once naturalistic and imaginative. In 1808, Turner became a founder-member of the longest-lived of these societies, "The Society for Epic and Pastoral Design". Although a member for only a few weeks, his work bears witness to the dual inheritance typified by the early work of Varley and Havell. (See fig.4, directly comparable to work produced by the Society.)

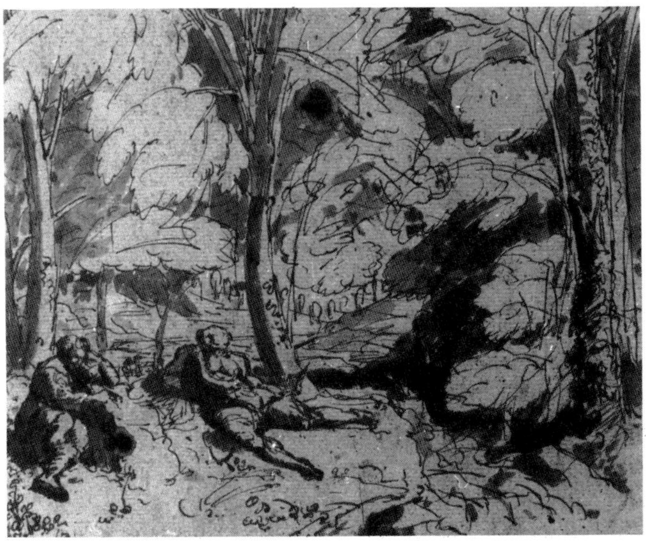

Fig. 3 *Retirement* c.1808? pen and ink and wash. Huntington Library, San Marino, California

In one particularly important respect the work produced by the Sketching Societies demonstrated the creative application of their direct contact with nature; this was in their attention to varying effects of light. Two of the Society's most favoured poets were Milton and Thompson, and this was no accident, for if Milton portrayed the imagery of light and darkness in all its cosmic power, it was Thompson, of all the eighteenth-century poets, who studied the fall of natural light, and indeed every type of meteorological effect, on the English landscape.

As interest in landscape shifted away from the classical, essentially timeless, ideal of Claude, carefully observed skies did as much as any other feature to create an atmosphere of historical specificity. The cloud sutdies of Constable may be the best known examples of their type, but they bear witness to a trend that was extremely widespread. The identification of many individual cloud types, and their relation to prevailing weather conditions, allowed the sky to become a bearer of more specific meanings within the landscape, extending its traditional function as a source of light.[11]

The success of William Turner's skies was commented on in his first exhibited works, and in some of his last, so that Ruskin's "look at the rolling clouds in Mr. Turner's *Ben Cruachan*, which are the finest clouds in the whole room", written in 1859, only echoes a review of 1808: "By the mere dint of his superior art he has rolled such clouds over these landscapes, as has given to a flat country an equal grandeur with mountain scenery.[12] At a time when the depiction of transitory effects became commonplace, Turner was one of the most insistent in describing the sky in the title of his pictures. He wanted to draw attention to it, reinforcing the image with the written word. By fixing the viewer in a particular moment, he sought to render the flight of the imagination all the more stimulating.

Turner's refusal to succumb to the generalising tendency of Varley's *Treatise* is evident in every area of his work. Writing of Pastoral Landscape, Varley advises "with respect to the general embellishments of landscape, there are few incidents which are equal to a flock of sheep . . .; and nothing gives a greater beauty to light and yellow greens, or burnt grass, than the introduction of white objects". For

Varley, as for Cox or Copley Fielding, the Pastoral demands a flock of sheep. Turner, however, sees not "embellishment", or "white objects"; he seems to perceive the human lot of the shepherd, and in his self-sufficiency finds an image of the free human spirit. Thus on the South Downs, or on Bullingdon Green, near Oxford, five or six small flocks are found in the same view, drawing attention at once to the extent of the provision of the open land, and the separate identity of the individual units.

Their timeless appearance allows the imagination to range without interference, promoting, as it does in Thompson, the sense of an enduring harmony between the landscape and its inhabitants. In the mid nineteenth century this harmony was in many respects an anachronism; enclosure, drainage and competitive breeding all threatened the traditional position of the shepherd. Turner refuses to acknowledge these developments. While large areas of Salisbury Plain were being given to the plough, at considerable capital cost, it remains for Turner a wasteland controlled only by elemental forces. Cotman's *Mousehold Heath* (1810), showing another ancient common with one encroaching strip of ploughed land, discusses the same issue with greater honesty.[13]

If sheep represented the old order on Salisbury Plain, they emphatically did not do so in the Highlands. It is no surprise, therefore, to find sheep almost completely absent from Turner's Highland views, while cattle and their drovers are a recurrent feature. The introduction of sheep farming to the Highlands, and the wholesale clearance of land once devoted to a cottage economy was destroying a way of life established for centuries. Other artists, Landseer and Copley Fielding among them, frequently included mixed herds of cattle and sheep in their Scottish pictures, whereas in Turner the sheep are conspicuous by their absence. The cattle droves were a commonplace in nineteenth-century art and literature about Scotland, encapsulating, as Dorothy Wordsworth put it, "the soul, the spirit, and solitary simplicity of many a Highland region."[14]

The theme, therefore, has historic and contemporary implications, and is essentially no different to that developed in many other areas.

It is not the attention to the human values represented by the figures in his landscapes, nor even the atmospheric excellence of the skies, in an age when cloud-painting became a commonplace pursuit, which are so impressive in Turner's work; it is the studied interdependence of all the individual elements of the painting built into a single whole. His primary concern is to articulate the meaning of a landscape and this is an attitude directly reflected in his style. The handling, which might appear laborious, lacking the fluidity so prized in the most admired masters of watercolour, J.M.W. Turner, Cox or DeWint, suggests a passionate attachment to his subjects, which he aims to present with the greatest possible definition. Whether painting scenes from his native Oxfordshire or the Highlands of Scotland, Turner never fails to convey a sense of personal involvement and his desire to grasp the essence of the subject which, for him, consists not only in the faithful rendering of material detail, the historically specific, but also in the exploration of its wider implications through the imagination.

Notes

1. For a full account of the history of the Society, see J.L. Roget, *A History of the Old Watercolour Society*, 2 vols, 1891, and J. Bayard, *From Drawing to Painting: The Exhibition Watercolour 1770–1870, PhD.*, Yale University, 1982.
2. See, for instance, M. Hardie, *Watercolour Painting in Britain*, III p.235.
3. A. Alison, *Essays on the Nature and Principles of Taste*, p.30–31.
4. Quoted by A. Hemingway, *Meaning in Cotman's Norfolk Subjects*, *Art History*, Vol.7 no.1, March 1984, p.61.
5. See J. Barrell, *The Idea of Landscape and the Sense of Place*, p.144.
6. W. Gilpin, *Remarks on Forest Scenery*, 3rd ed., 1808, p.219–20.
7. See B. Reaney, *The Class Struggle in 19th Century Oxfordshire. The social and communal background to the Otmoor disturbances of 1830 to 1835*, History Workshop Pamphlets 3, 1970.
8. *A Handbook to the Watercolours, Drawings and Engravings in the Art Treasures Exhibition, being a reprint of critical notices originally published in 'The Manchester Guardian'*, 1857, p.37.
9. See Norwich, Castle Museum, *A Decade of English Naturalism, 1810–1820* exhibition catalogue by J. Gage, 1969.
10. See J. Hamilton, *The Sketching Society*, Victoria and Albert Museum, 1971.
11. See particularly T. Forster, *Researches into Atmospheric Phenomena*, 3rd revised ed., 1823 and L. Hawes *Constable's Sky Sketches*, Journal of the Warburg and Courtauld Institutes XXXII, 1969.
12. Both quoted in M. Hardie, *William Turner of Oxford, (1789–1862) Old Watercolour Society's Club*, Annual Volume IX, 1931–32, p.2 and p.6.
13. Arts Council of Great Britain, *John Sell Cotman, 1782–1842*, 1982–83 Cat.80, repr. in colour.
14. Quoted in K.J. Bonser, *The Drovers*, p.24.

Turner's Patrons

The Watercolour Society was the first exhibiting body in London to keep a price-book for the registration of paintings sold at the annual exhibition. These books almost all survive, and provide an invaluable record of the type of patronage the watercolourists attracted. In addition, Turner's own catalogues of the exhibitions survive in the Library of the Victoria and Albert Museum. His marginal notes of purchasers, and occasional comments on the work of his fellows, make them the single most valuable document of his career.[1] Close inspection reveals that some of the notes of buyers must have been recorded from memory, sometimes several years after the event.

In its early years, the Watercolour Society attracted buyers from among the wealthiest collectors in the country, including the Marquis of Stafford, the Earl of Essex and the Earl of Tankerville, who all bought extensively, and Turner benefitted from the general trend. Two of the most important collectors of watercolours, Dr Monro and Walter Fawkes, who patronised most of the Society's members, do not appear to have bought works by Turner; John Allnutt, however, who built up one of the greatest collections of English painting of the first half of the century, bought the large, important composition *Evening* in 1813, now unfortunately in a ruinous condition (Sotheby's, 20 July 1978, lot 164). At the later London exhibitions, there was an irregular trickle of aristocratic clients; Lord Portman acquired works in 1835 and 1845 and Lady Trevelyan of Wallington in Northumberland, the patroness of some of the Pre-Raphaelite circle, bought in 1836 and 1849; the Duke of Devonshire, not otherwise known as a buyer of watercolours, acquired a small view of Stonehenge in 1838. His purchase throws an interesting sidelight on Samuel Palmer's anxiety to tap this source at around the same date; "if I could but get at the affections of the Dukes of Sutherland or Devonshire . . . what a merry little Falstaff I should be!" (to John Linnell, 16 December 1838).[2] The Duke of Sutherland was also a buyer of Turner's, purchasing a watercolour of *Cherwell Water-Lilies* in 1846.

Turner does not appear to have built up any special relationship with any collectors in London. In Oxford his prospects might have appeared even more limited but he did have a certain local following and a virtual monopoly of the market, such as it was. Several masters and fellows of the colleges bought works; of the many clergymen who bought the occasional watercolour at the London exhibitions, only one was not an Oxford man.

It seems that only the wealthiest of Oxford families bought with any regularity. Turner's bankers, the Thompson family, owned several works, the earliest being the view of Glencoe acquired from the SPW in 1839 (Cat.62). The work had personal interest for them, depiciting a site close to family estates in the Highlands, a consideration important to many, if not all, buyers. Other Thompson purchases included several views of Oxford, and a group depicting the family seat of Woodperry.[3] The two names appearing most often as buyers at the London exhibitions are Morrell and Wyatt. It was the wife of Baker Morrell, solicitor to the University (the grandfather of Lady Ottoline) whose first purchase is recorded in 1818; others followed, stretching into the 1840s. The collection of Oxfordshire views built up by Edward Parker Morrell (1839–1908), sold after the death of his widow from the family house of Black Hall in St Giles in 1925, included probably the largest group of Turner's work ever assembled, but apart from the few works which descended through the family the majority were acquired from various sources after Turner's death. The activities of James Wyatt (1774–1853) as a publisher of prints and a picture dealer made him the most important figure in the artistic life of Oxford. In 1809 he commissioned two large oils of Oxford from J.M.W. Turner which he subsequently published, and in the 1840's he became the first patron of the teenage Millais. He bought from Turner throughout his career, but kept only two relatively slight examples for his own extensive collection (his sale, Christie's 4 July 1853, lots 353 and 410). His son, James Wyatt Junior, continued his business, and was the principal buyer at Turner's studio sale in 1863; Wyatt Junior's obituary in *The Times* makes special mention of his friendship with the painter (15 August 1882).

Notes

1. These notes are transcribed by Hardie, Old Watercolour Society's Club Annual Vol. IX, 1931–32.
2. R. Lister Ed., *The Letters of Samuel Palmer*, Oxford 1974, vol.1. p.257.
3. See *View from the Garden*, repr. *Country Life* CXIX, 5 January 1961, p.21.

Select Bibliography

Abbreviations used in the catalogue in bold type
Place of publication is London, unless otherwise stated

Alison, Archibald. Essay on the Nature and Principles of Taste. Edinburgh, 1790.

Arts Council of Great Britain. John Sell Cotman. Exhibition catalogue, 1982.

Baldry, A.L. William Turner of Oxford, Water-Colour Painter. Walker's Quarterly, 1923.

Barrell, John. The idea of Landscape and the sense of place. Cambridge, 1972.

Bayard, Jane. Works of Splendor and Imagination: the Exhibition Watercolour, 1770–1870. New Haven, 1981.

Bonser, K.J. The Drovers. 1970.

Bovill, E.W. English Country Life, 1780–1830. 1926.

Cohn, M.B. Wash and gouache. A Study of the Development of the Materials of Watercolour. Fogg Art Museum, Cambridge, Mass., 1977.

Emery, Frank. The Oxfordshire Landscape. 1974.

Hamilton, Jean. The Sketching Society, 1799–1851. Victoria and Albert Museum, 1971.

Hardie, Martin. Water-colour Painting in Britain. II. The Romantic Period. 1967.

Hardie, Martin. William Turner of Oxford, Old Watercolour Society's Club, Annual Volume IX, 1931–1932.

Heleniak, K.M. William Mulready. 1980.

Herrmann, Luke. William Turner of Oxford. Connoisseur, vol. CLXII, August 1966, pp. 242–247.

Holloway, James, and Lindsay Errington. The Discovery of Scotland. National Gallery of Scotland, Edinburgh, 1978.

Hubbard, Hesketh. "The Society for the Study of Epic and Pastoral Design". Old Watercolour Society's Club, Annual Volume XXIV, 1946.

Hayes, John. The Landscape Paintings of Thomas Gainsborough, 1982.

London, Spink & Son. William Havell. Exhibition catalogue, 1981.

Murdoch, John. Forty-two British Watercolours from the Victoria and Albert Museum. 1977.

Nicolson, Marjorie Hope. Mountain gloom and mountain glory. Ithaca, New York, 1959.

Price, Uvedale. An Essay on the Picturesque. 1794.

Roget, J.L. A History of the Old Watercolour Society. 1891.

Ruskin, John. Modern Painters. 1843–1860.

Smith, Hammond. Peter DeWint. 1982.

Taylor, Basil. Joshua Cristall. Victoria and Albert Museum, 1975.

Vainker, Philip. Art Criticism and Art Reviewing, 1780–1830. Unpublished M.A. Report, Courtauld Institute of Art, 1977.

Wilton, Andrew. British Watercolours 1750–1850. Oxford, 1977.

Catalogue

Abbreviations

Exh:	Exhibited
Prov:	Provenance
Ref:	References
Repr.	Reproduced
SPW	The Royal Society of Painters in Watercolours
Studio sale	Christie's, 9 March 1862, *Catalogue of the remaining work of . . . W. Turner*
UG	University Galleries, Oxford, *Exhibition of the work of William Turner*, 1895.

All watercolours have pencil underdrawing, unless stated otherwise
Titles of works known to have been exhibited by the artist are given in their original form
Dimensions are given in centimetres, height before width

1. 1789–1811

William Turner was born on 12 November 1789 at Black Bourton in Oxfordshire. His father Robert was from Burford, his mother Mary (née Cox, born 6 January 1767) was from the parish of Black Bourton. They married on 13 August 1789 in her home parish and William was the first of their three children. He had two sisters, Anne Cox (baptised 1 June 1791) and Margot (baptised 13 May, 1792); the youngest of his sisters was born fatherless, for the register of burials records Robert Turner's interment at Black Bourton on 5 September 1791. It is not certain how long the family remained together. Perhaps Mary Turner did manage to raise the children together until 1803, when it seems that William, then fourteen, was sent to live with the prosperous uncle after whom he had been named. William Turner, Senior (1756–1853) of Burford, had, in that same year, purchased the Manor House and the entire parish of Shipton-upon-Cherwell, near Woodstock. The whole estate consisted of 537 acres and was either freehold, or on lease from New College, Oxford. The purchase price was probably something in the region of £10,000 (a mortgage was obtained from the Duke of Malborough for £9,900).

It may be that Turner's early attempts with the brush (see Cat.3) suggested an artistic career as a possibility. At this point it seems likely that the uncle may have taken advice from William Delamotte (1775–1863) who in 1798 had inherited John Baptiste Malchair's practice as drawing-master among the undergraduates in the city. The evidence of the early sketchbook (see Cat.10) would seem to indicate that some contact, possibly formal lessons, was arranged. Sometime in 1803 Delamotte left Oxford to become second drawing-master at the Royal Military Academy, Great Marlow; it may have been on his advice that Turner was placed with John Varley in London in 1804.

It is impossible to be certain whether this was a formal apprenticeship, but certainly by the summer of that year he was living at Varley's address in Broad Street, Golden Square. He gives this as his residence at his first exhibition at the Royal Academy in 1807; given the fact of his wealthy background and Varley's reputation as a teacher it is reasonable to suppose that a binding financial deal would have been struck. It is perhaps significant in this connection that seven years later when he came of age Turner returned to Oxford. Of his two fellow-pupils who also exhibited at this 1807 exhibition, William Henry Hunt and John Linnell, Hunt gives Varley's as his address, but Linnell gives an address in Bloomsbury.

Turner's relationship with the two younger boys is problematic. In Linnell's *Autobiographical Notes* (Linnell family collection) Turner is not mentioned at all; he writes of this period 1805–7: "Hunt and I were always out, weather permitted, painting in oil on millboard from nature". The evidence is, however, that Turner did in fact, accompany the two on some occasions though perhaps their friendship was not close, Hunt and Linnell being a couple of years younger at a time when such small differences matter. Linnell is at pains in the *Notes* to point out that, despite being Varley's official students, their main influence was from Mulready, Varley's young brother-in-law. This influence is readily apparent in Turner's *Riverbank* (Cat.7) which directly parallels the innovative oils of Mulready in its adoption of a high horizon. Moreover, the three are recorded as a group by Edward Monro in the diaries he kept whilst living with his father Dr Thomas Monro, the "mental physician" who treated John Robert Cozens and was the patron of J.M.W. Turner and Girtin. Varley also received his patronage and it is he who must have introduced his pupils to Monro, who was then living at Bushey. Edward Monro's entries are usually taken to refer to J.M.W. Turner but it seems unlikely that the artist should be referred to in the same sentence as two boys of fifteen or thereabouts. We find in April 1806 "Linnell, Hunt and Turner to draw" and the same in December 1806. Monro's collection of the old and modern masters was extensive, as were his connections. Edward records for example, on 3 November 1809 "Lord Essex and Mr Turner called"; the 5th Earl was a patron of both Turners (in 1808 he bought J.M.W. Turner's *Purfleet* from the Turner Gallery and in the same year *On the River Cherwell* from SPW). It is impossible to be certain which Turner Monro refers to here. While the elder Turner is far the more likely candidate, it is important to note that Monro could provide introductions to the class of patron that William Turner was beginning to attract at this date.

In 1808 he was elected an Associate of the SPW (at seventeen, its youngest member) and in November of the same year a full member. In January 1808 he became one of the founder members of the reformed Sketching Society, *The Society for Epic and Pastoral Design* (see Cat.8), and presided at the first meeting. On the 27th of the same month the Royal Academician and diarist Joseph Farington was at a gathering of a number of leading artists, and recorded that "Varley spoke violently of the merit of a young man who has been his Pupil in learning to draw in watercolour and Reinagle said 'He had never before seen drawings equal to them'. His name Turner." John Landseer writing in *The Review of Publications of Art* (September 1808) goes further. He observes that Turner "is following hard after Callcott and Havell and his own great namesake. His CORN-FIELD near WOODSTOCK, his

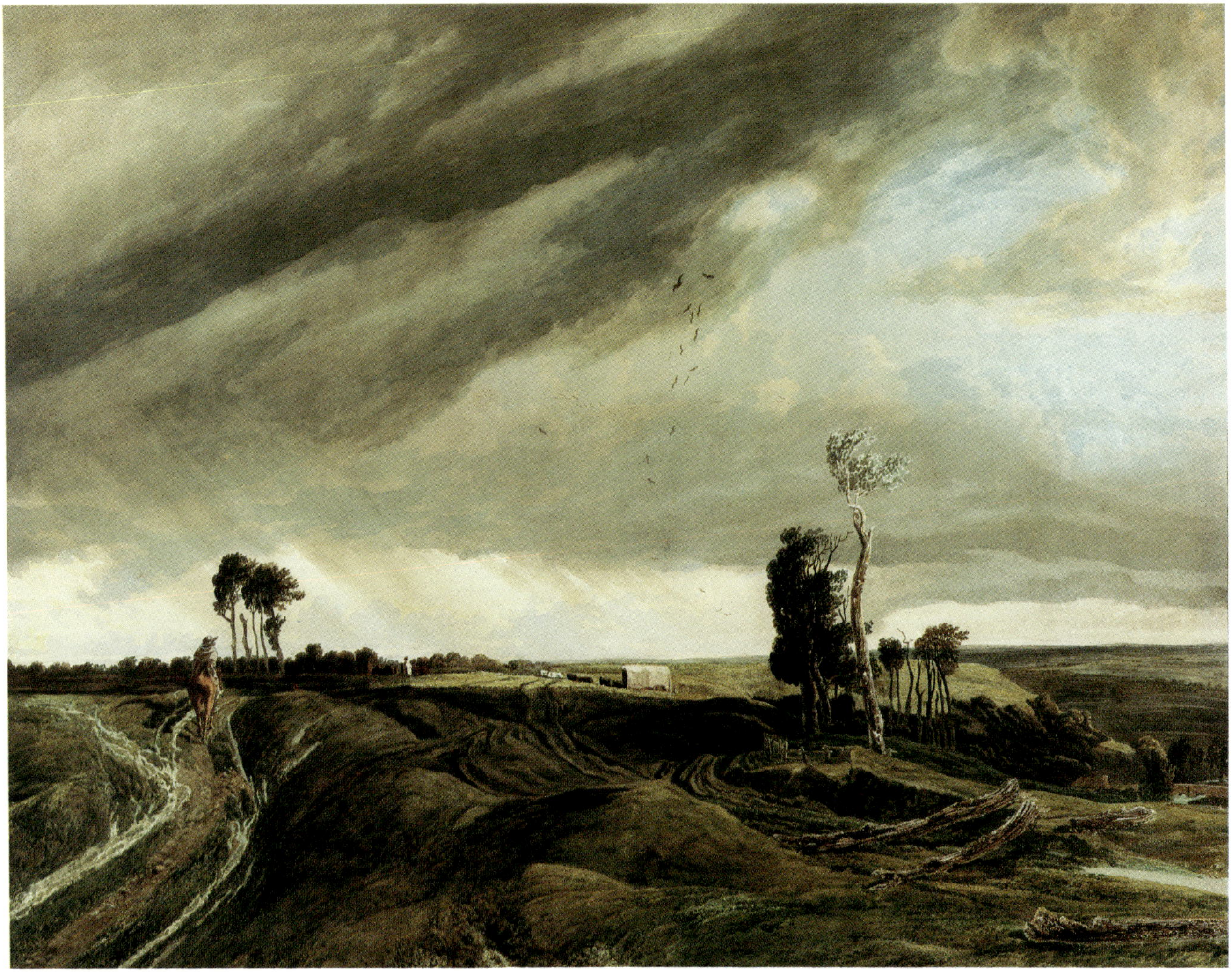

Cat.13: **Scene near Woodstock**

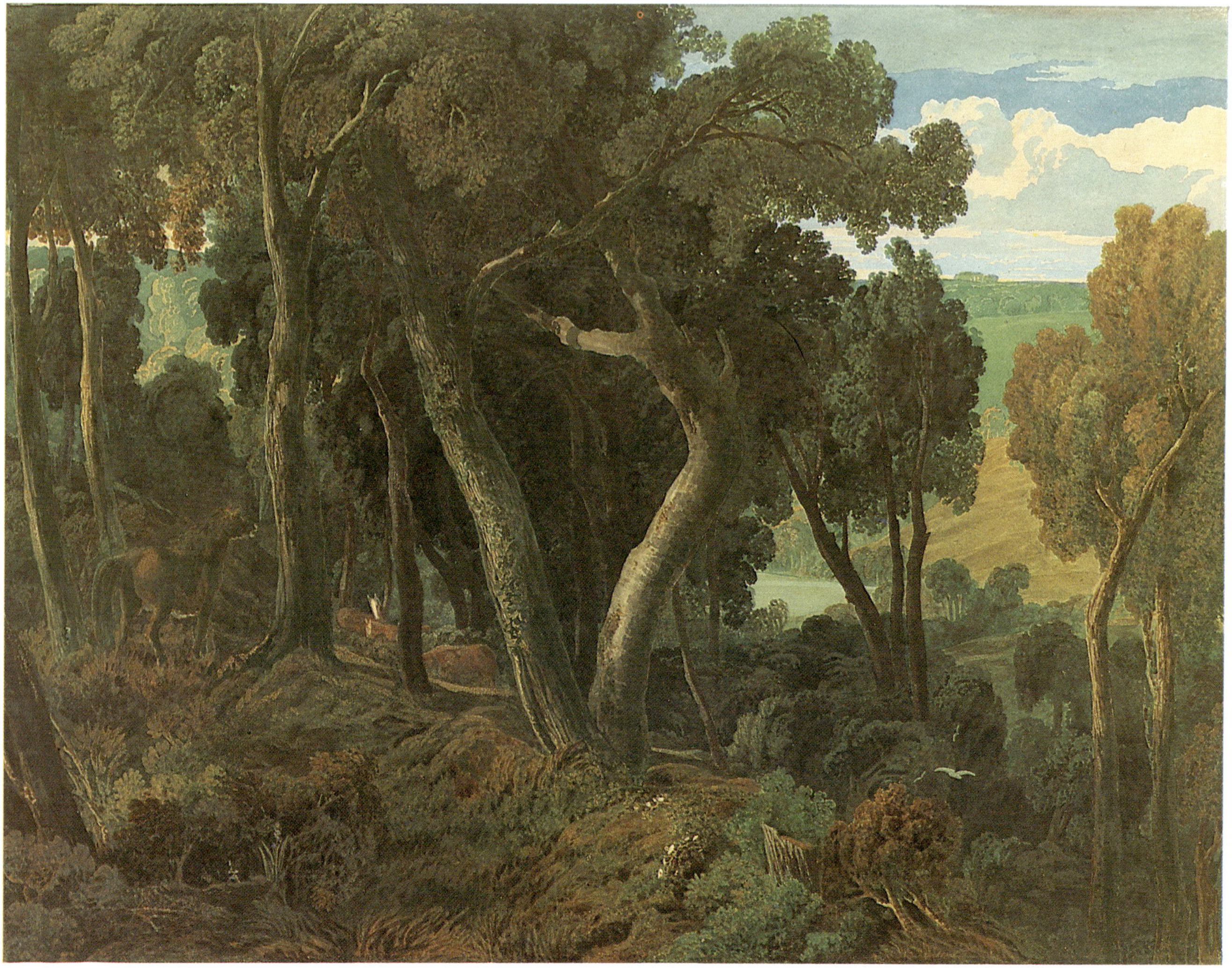

***Cat.14*: Whichwood Forest, Oxfordshire**

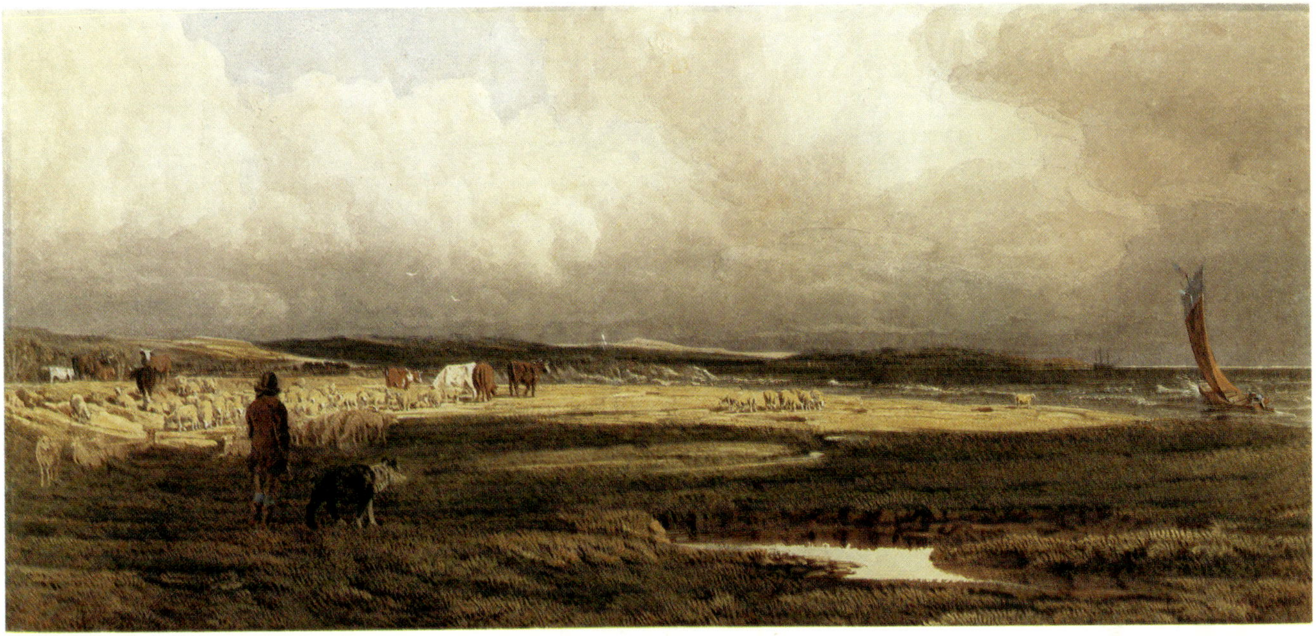

Cat.18: **View from a Salt Marsh near Shirehampton, Gloucestershire**

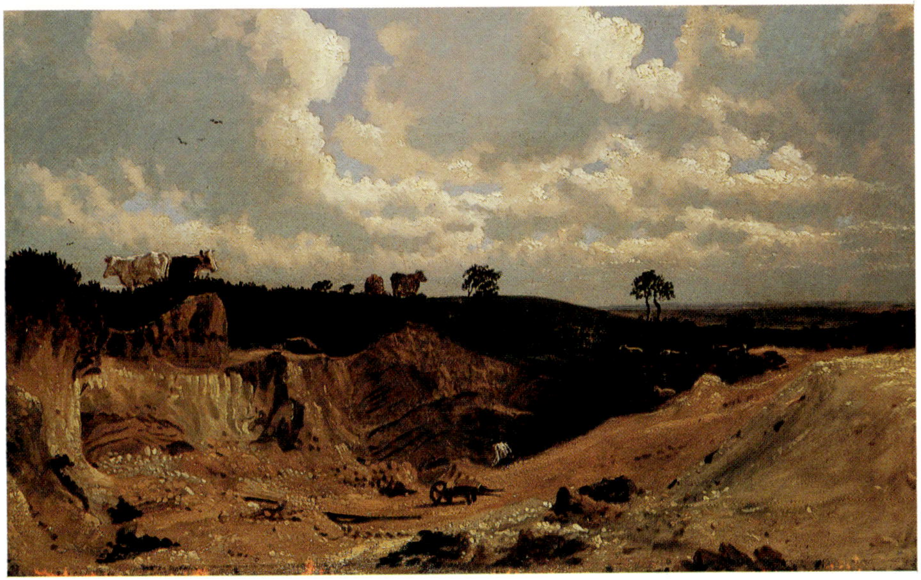

Cat.36: **Pit on Shotover Hill**

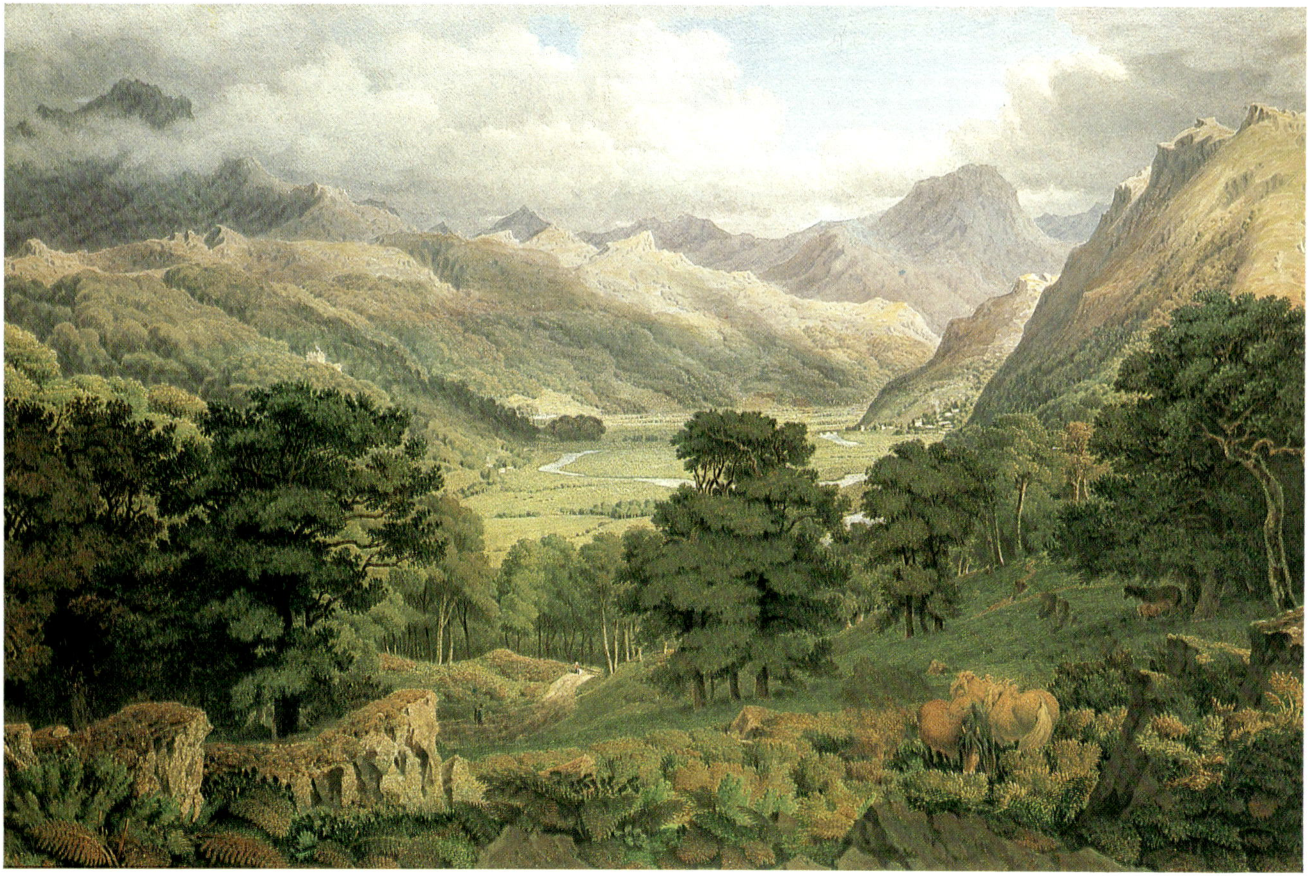

***Cat.31*: The Vale of Ffestiniog**

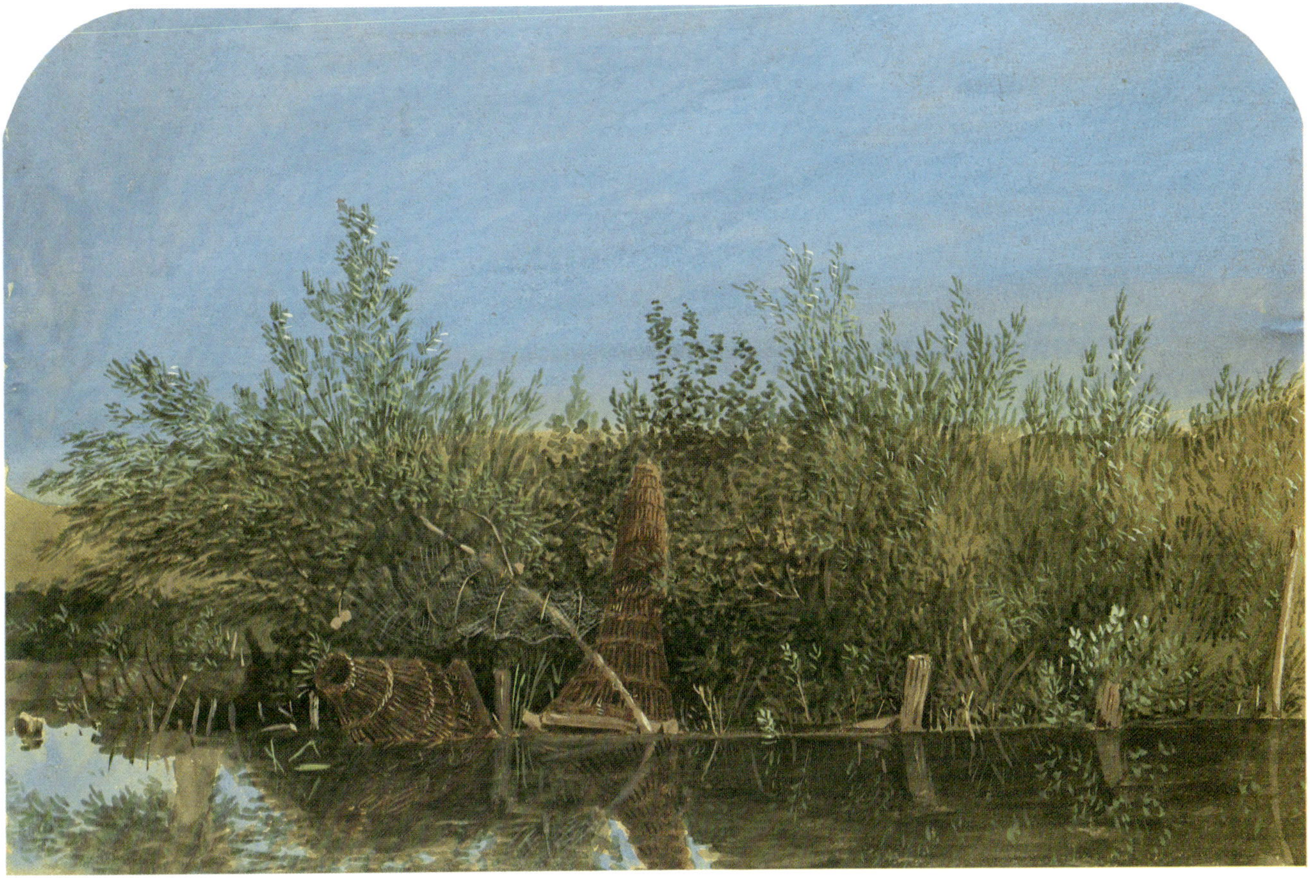

Cat.56: **Eel Traps on the Cherwell**

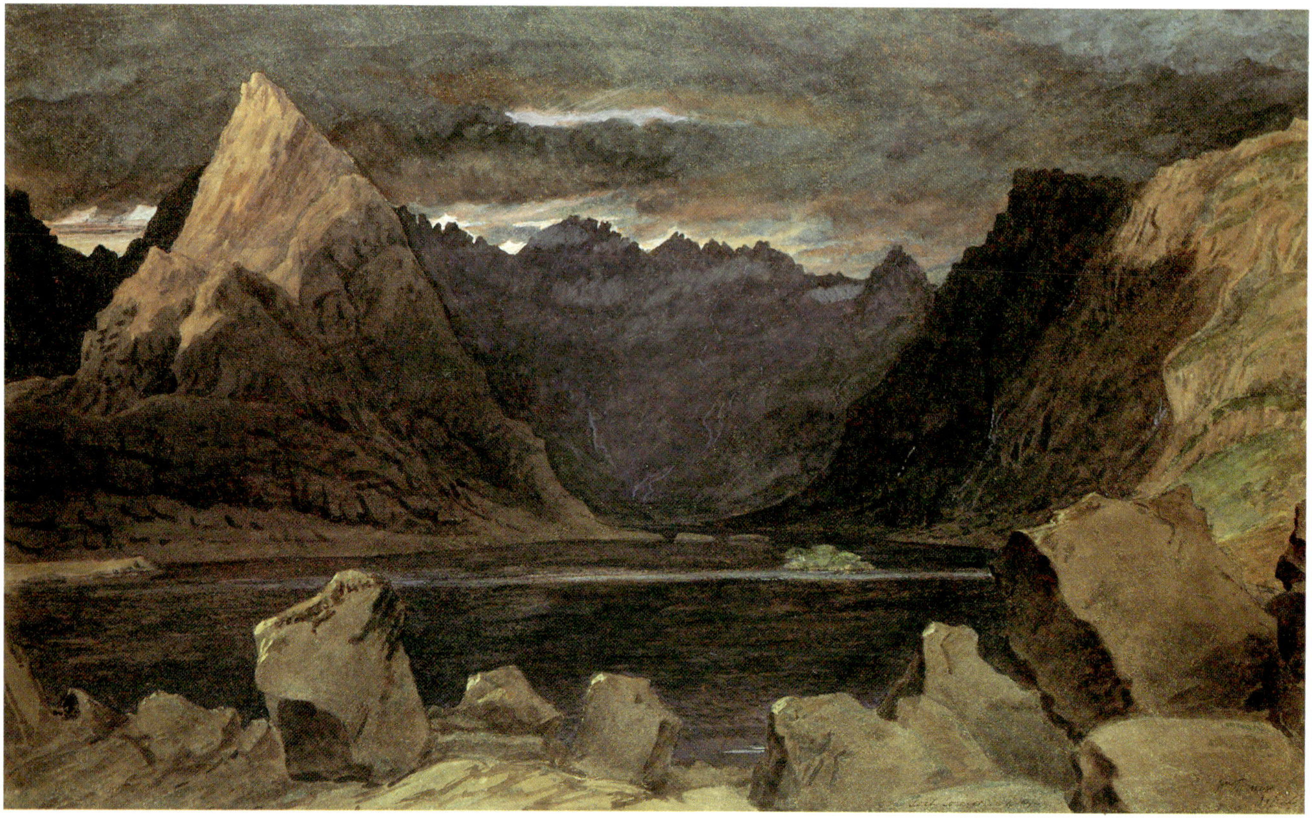

***Cat.61*: Loch Coruisk, Isle of Skye, at Sunset**

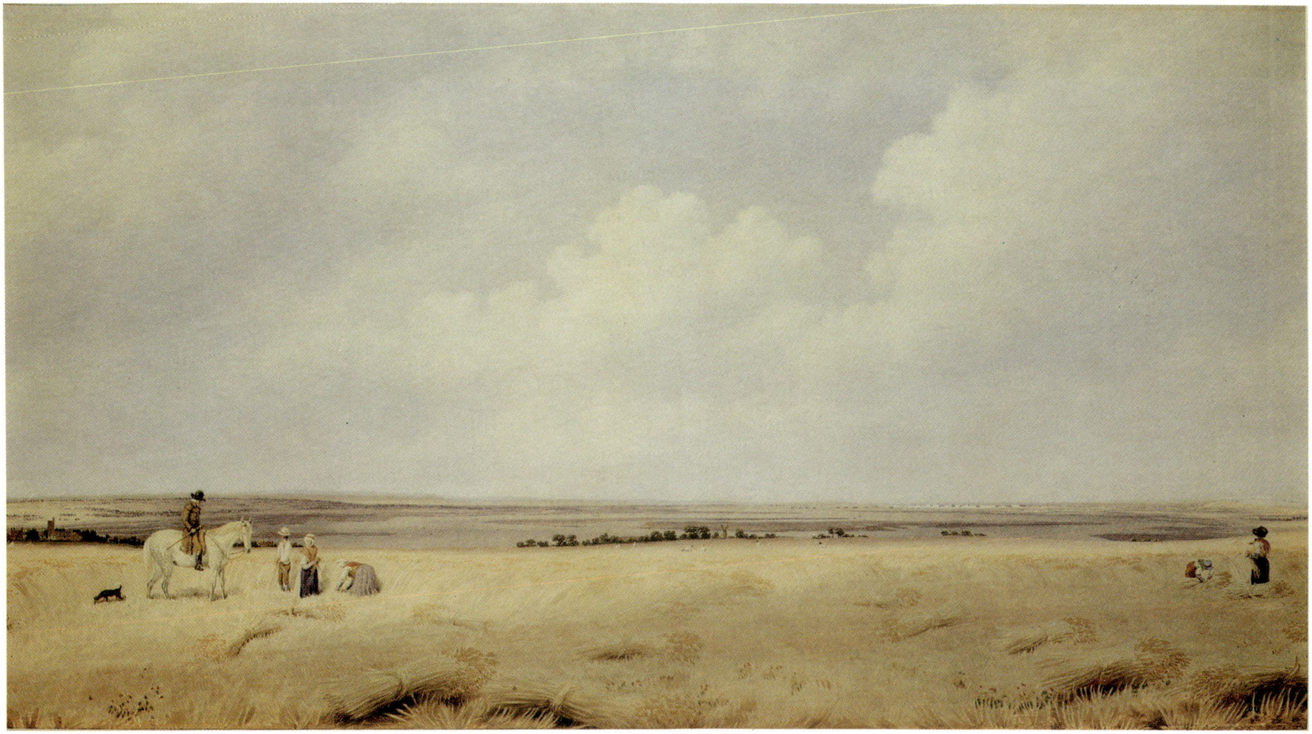

Cat.68: **View from Bow Hill on the South Downs near Chichester – Langston and Portsmouth Harbour, and the Isle of Wight in the distance**

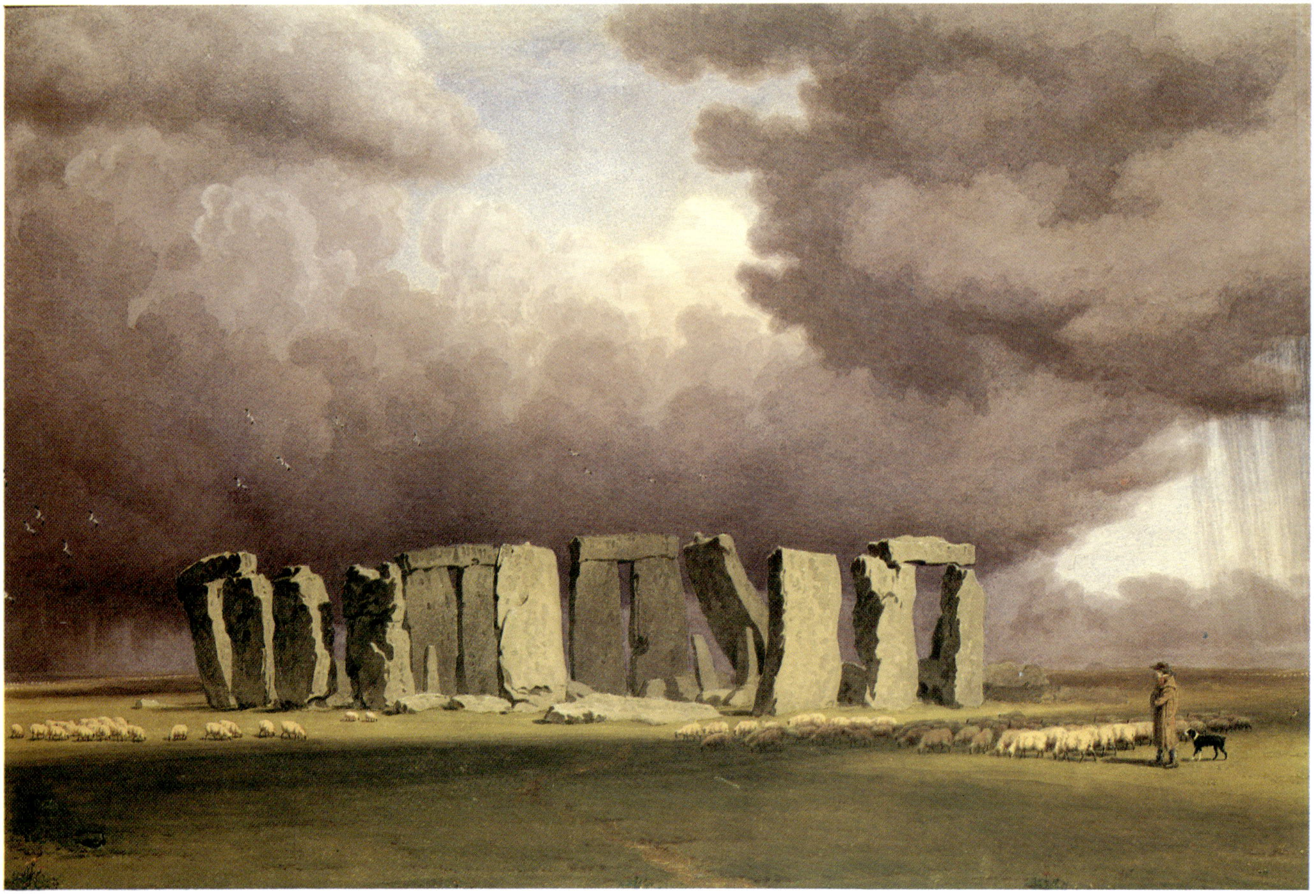

Cat.69: **Stonehenge, stormy day**

OTTMOOR, and his WHICHWOOD FOREST (all in Oxfordshire) display the wide range of capacity and contrivance, of a veteran landscape painter . . . So very far are these performances of Mr Turner from discovering any traits of the timidity and temerity of youth, that were we not well informed that their author is a young man, we should have concluded he was an artist of long practice, and of judgement matured by age." Landseer was responding to the scale, the finish and the sonorous and grave colouring which he equates with serious and important public address (see Cat.13 and 14).

Despite the fact that he was now based in London, his first exhibited pictures are of the familiar locations of his childhood. The first indications of a trip further afield come in 1808 when he travelled to Lancashire, possibly at the invitation of Thomas Lister Parker of Browsholme Hall, a patron of J.M.W. Turner. He does not seem to have broadened or extended this visit to take in the Lake District, and the only two subjects that document the trip are depictions of scenes which lie within a mile or two of the Hall. The first major tour was made either in 1808 or in the following year, initially to Bristol and Cheltenham. In 1808, Turner sold a watercolour to C.J. Harford of Bristol, and the connection may have inspired the visit. In view of the romantic associations of the forest of Wychwood (see Cat.14) it is significant to find Turner at the same moment investigating scenery which pre-eminently deserved the same epithet. Farington records on 28 February 1808 "Fuseli was last week at Clifton near Bristol and raved abt. the romantic scenery, saying 'it was the first thing in the Kingdom, Sublime &c'.".

By way of contrast, the tour was extended into the Wye valley and Chepstow, the area eulogised in the Rev. William Gilpin's first tour (*Observations on the River Wye*, 1782), and then the heartland of the popular Picturesque.

The many sketches and related drawings he made around this date are to a large extent preserved in three albums now in the Henry E. Huntington Museum and Library in San Marino, California. The drawings they contain date from c.1805–22 and range through copies of Raphael and Girtin, to direct studies from nature and a series (c.1810) which experiments with the transfiguring properties of light or "effect" over a single given subject. They give the clearest indication of the eclecticism of these early years and also of Turner's confidence in extemporising landscape subjects on the basis of his study "in the field" (see figs.3 and 4).

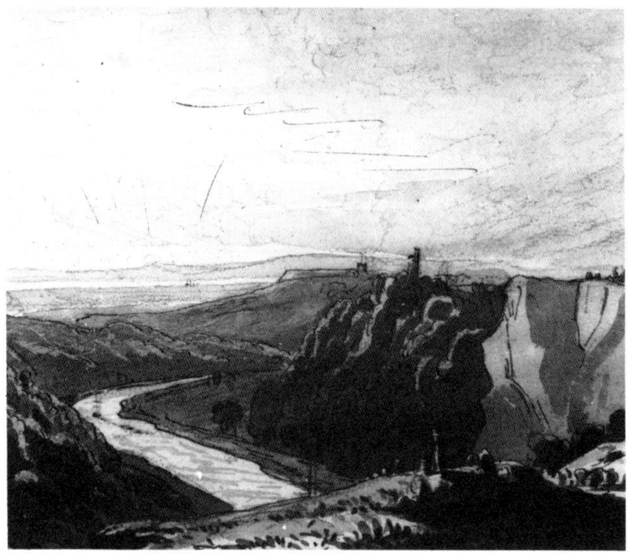

Fig. 4 *Durdham Down* c.1808–10? Pencil and wash. Huntington Library, San Marino, California

1 Old Manor House, Shipton-on-Cherwell, Oxford, 1805

1805
Pencil on flecked cream wove
21.7 × 39
Signed *W. T. Oxford*; and inscribed with title, and dated *1805*.

Prov: Colnaghi's, 1959.

The manor is seen distantly across one of his uncle's fields. Most of Turner's attention, however, has been taken by the corn-stooks. The subject was to become one of the staples of the next two decades, particularly in the work of DeWint. At this date, however, such a scene was unusual, the more so for the complete absence of reapers or gatherers either at rest or hard at work. Graphically, the subject offered an opportunity to demonstrate virtuoso pencil work; Turner makes good use of it, inscribing bundles of strongly hatched lines that, in their contrasting directions not only give the picture an interesting surface rhythm, but articulate an expanse rhythmically punctuated by a series of uprights.

Collection of Nicholas and Susan Thomas

2a William Turner, Lord of the Manor, and a lady on horseback

(c.1805?)
Pencil with white bodycolour on grey wove cartridge
26.4 × 24.3

2b Two women on horseback

(c.1805?)
Pencil with white bodycolour on grey wove cartridge
26.5 × 18.2
Both inscribed verso *Oxford by/ William Turner*

The Visitors of the Ashmolean Museum, Oxford

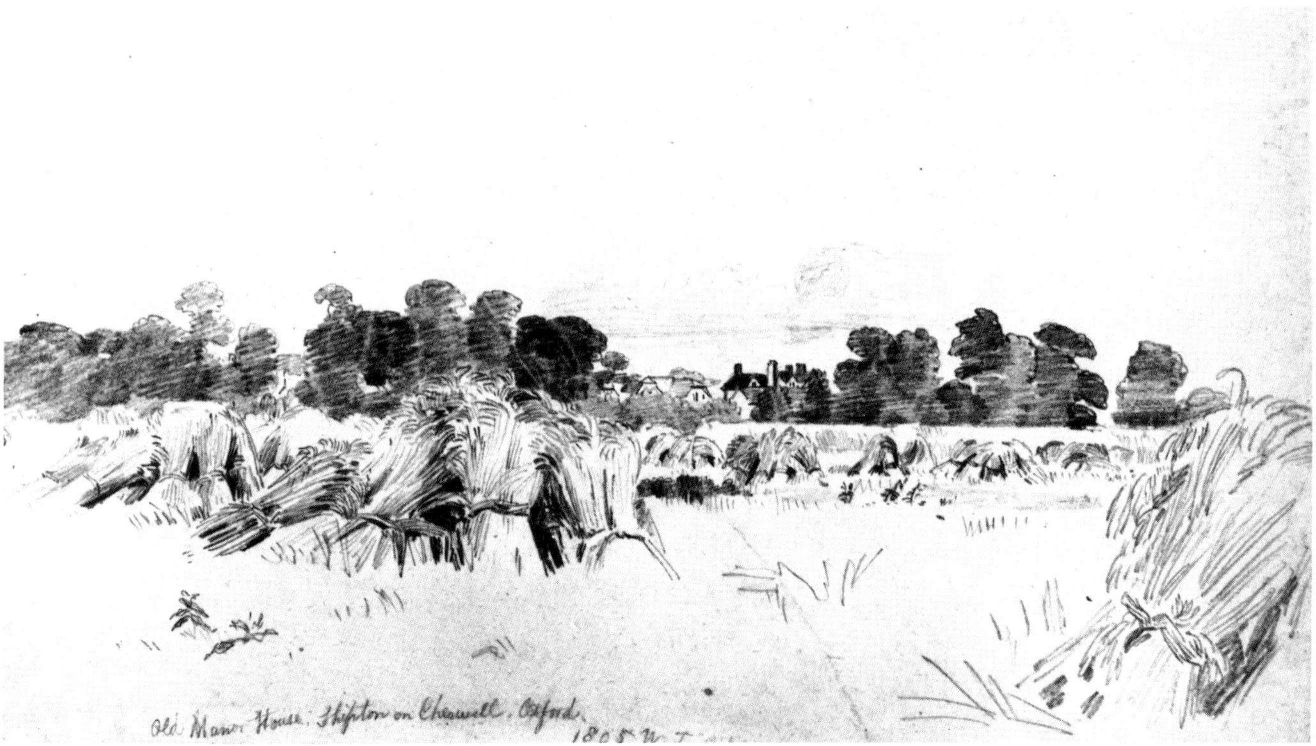

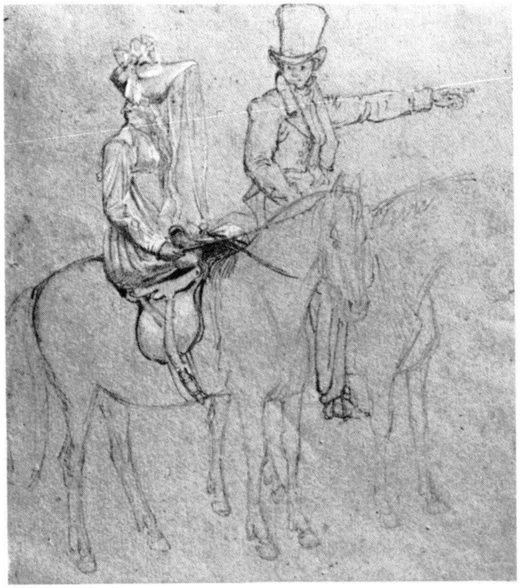

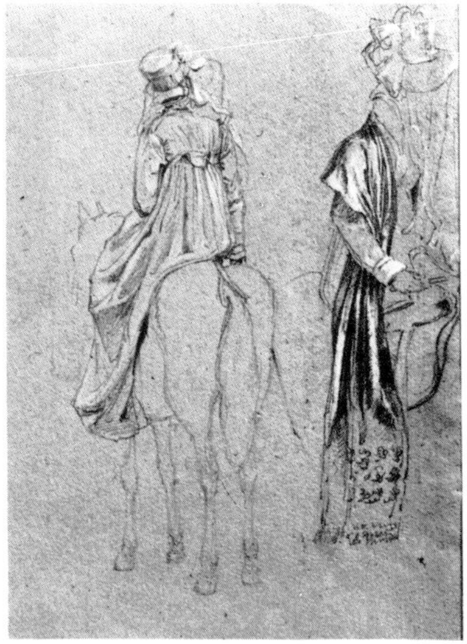

Cat.2a and 2b

3 William Turner, Lord of the Manor, and two women on horseback

(c.1805?)
Oil on millboard
13.5 × 16.1
Inscribed verso by a nineteenth-century descendant *[Ascen]sion Day/[ske]tch by Wm. Turner, date probably [?some time] before he took up his [residence at] Shipton-on-Cherwell with/Wm. Turner Esq. Lord o[f the Man]or/the figures doubt[less]/Wm. Turner aforesaid and two of/[his ?daughters or ?cousins] Mary and Fanny.*

Prov: Presumably William Turner Senior; by descent.

Together, these related studies represent some of Turner's earliest surviving work. The inscription on the little oil study, based on later guesswork by a member of the family, is on the whole misleading. Turner's uncle purchased Shipton Manor in 1803, and the young Turner appears to have gone to live there very soon afterwards. The immature handling of the paint in the oil sketch makes an early date feasible, but probably nearer to 1805, which is a couple of years later than is implied by the inscription. The direct observation of the figures in the pencil drawings surely precedes their inclusion in the sketch. These drawings, although weak in parts, are solid and confident for juvenile productions, and hardly less advanced than the drawing of the Manor dated 1805 (Cat. 1). Mary and Fanny were daughters of William Turner Senior, and William's cousins, but were not born until 1806 and 1812 respectively; the identity of the figures, who one might guess were all of roughly the same age, therefore remains problematic. Two of the mounted women, the nearer figure in each drawing, are reused in a much later watercolour inscribed *Scene near Malvern* (perhaps c.1830).

Mr and Mrs Robert Turner

4 Study of a tree

(datable 1806)
Lithograph
Image 33.7 × 21.3
Signed on image *W. Turner* and inscribed on stone *LONDON: printed from stone in the polyautographic office, No.9 Buckingham Place, Fitzroy Square.*

Prov: Purchased, 1870.
Ref: F.L. Emanuel, *Some remarks on early lithography*, *Print Collectors' Quarterly XXI*, 1934, p.345, repr. p.340. F.H. Man, *Lithography in England 1800–1810*, in C. Zigrosser, *Prints*, 1963.

In the spring of 1806, the German G.J. Vollweiler, who held the English patent for the new process of lithography, issued circulars inviting

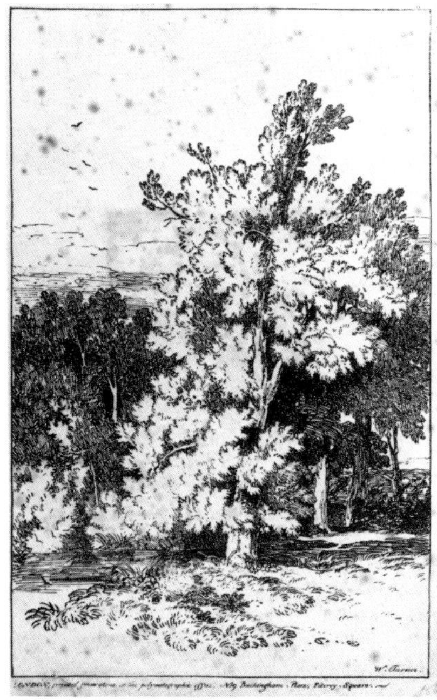

amateurs to try their hand at the art. This print of Turner's was almost certainly produced at that time.

Turner would undoubtedly have known of the process earlier; William Delamotte's first essays in the medium date back to 1801. It is Delamotte who provided the basis for Turner's graphic style here, not in lithography, but in the soft-ground etchings *Forest trees* published in 1804.

The Trustees of the British Museum

5 Standing Boy

(c.1806)
Black and white chalk on blue wove cartridge, the drawing gummed
20.5 × 11.7

Prov: Mr P.P. Rhodes, by whom presented, 1958.

Probably made in the early days of his apprenticeship to Varley (c.1806). There are a great many similar drawings by fellow-pupils John Linnell and William Henry Hunt, but the type is much rarer in Turner.

Aesthetically, the drawing clearly relates to the Picturesque; specifically, that propounded by Sir Uvedale Price. In his *Essays on the Picturesque* of 1794, Price notes the pleasing and beautiful properties of intricacy and variety produced in landscape and in the appearance of humans by neglect and the accidental effects of time: "In our own species, objects merely picturesque are to be found among the wandering tribes of gypsies and beggars; who in all the qualities which give them that character bear a close analogy to the wild forester and the worn out cart horse, and again to old mills, hovels, and other inanimate

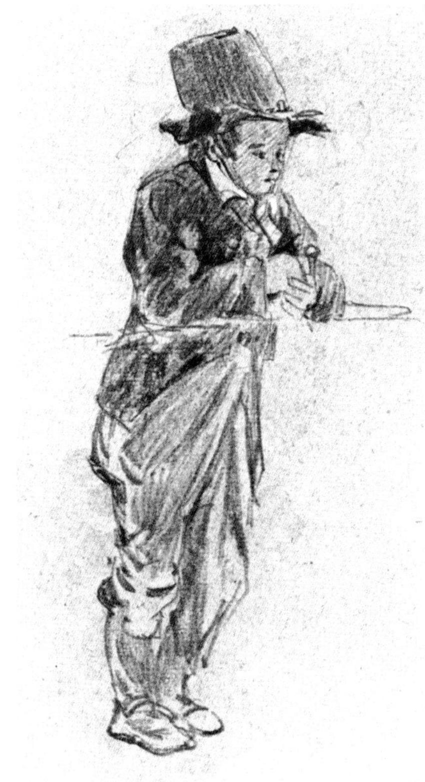

objects of the same kind."

Technically, the rough crumbling property of chalk is well-suited to the depiction of such qualities, as is the coarse impure paper.

In terms of subject matter, the boy himself, as a member of the labouring classes, was valued in the Picturesque. Such figures were not only appreciated aesthetically, but as exemplars of the organic unity of man in close touch with nature.

The Visitors of the Ashmolean Museum, Oxford

6 Two studies of a barge canopy and figures

(c.1806–7)
Black and white chalk on blue wove cartridge
23.7 × 42
Signed *W T.*

Prov: Sotheby's, 19 March 1981, lot 79 (part).

Contemporaries report that Varley's pupils would sit down "before any common object, the paling of a cottage garden or a mossy wall or an old post [and] try to imitate it minutely" (Roget, I, p.390). In particular, the studies made by William Henry Hunt and John Linnell in about 1806 of ramshackle fences and eel-pots (e.g. Hunt's *Study from Nature at Twickenham* and Linnell's *Twickenham*, both Tate Gallery) demonstrate not only a devotion to the accurate imitation of form and surface texture, but a keen eye for the play of light and its creation of pattern. These rudimentary constructs are shown to relate just as closely to their natural environment as to any idea of the human intervention implied in their making, and are thus fitting emblems of an art supposedly passively observed. The same quiet receptivity characterises Turner's pencil sketches of similar subjects, which may have been made in the company of the two boys. Here, the barges are appreciated for their structure: the joints, brackets and pegs which hold the vessel together and allow it to function. The drawing is analogous to an academic dissection study, Turner enjoying the way the

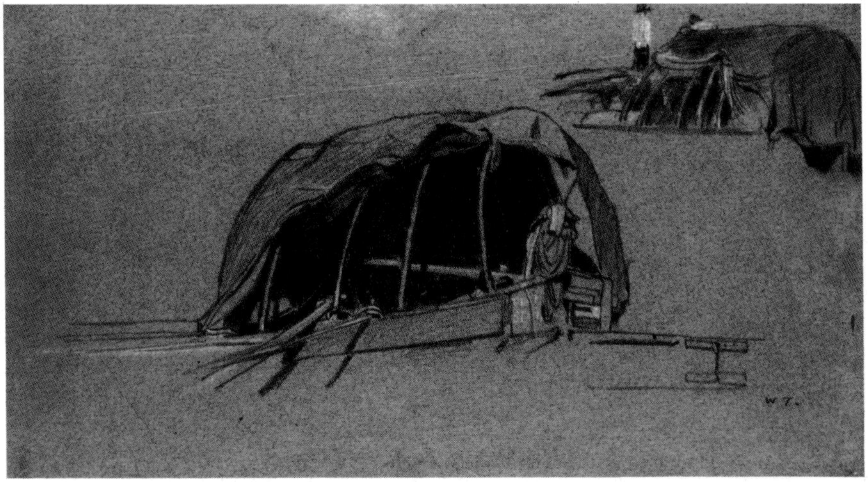

tarpaulin has been peeled back like a skin to reveal a rib-cage of poles and spars beneath.

Mr Nicholas Meinertzhagen

7 Riverbank

(c.1806–7)
Black and white chalk on blue laid cartridge
17.2 × 28
Signed in ink *W. Turner*

Prov: Sotheby's, 22 April 1982, lot 1; Cyril Fry; purchased, 1984 (VAM E.253-1984).

A drawing extracted from a folio (c.1806–10) that included studies by William Henry Hunt, John Linnell and John Varley. Inscriptions on some of them establish the folio as a collection probably made on teaching outings conducted by Varley in Bayswater and on Millbank. In point of fact, however, the present drawing resembles those *plein air* oils made by William Mulready (Varley's brother-in-law) on Hampstead Heath in 1806. (See particularly *Hampstead Heath*, K.M. Heleniak, *William Mulready*, 1982, pl.34). The varied textures of the "broken" ground and the crumbling and disintegrating sandy bank, have, like *Standing Boy* (Cat.5), obvious connections with the Priceian Picturesque. Here Turner confines himself to a close frame-filling foreground that rises quickly away from the viewer to silhouette a figure at its crest. The figure, thus treated, proclaims attachment to the masters of seventeenth-century Dutch landscape and predates the similar interests of the East Anglian School.

It is the declared confidence in the empirically knowable foreground that is of most interest here. In restricting our vision, Turner is implicitly rejecting the prospect view as relatively abstract and general. By turning our attention to what in the conventional prospect was of secondary interest, the particular, concrete details of nature, he is siding with those Naturalists who opposed the Academic-Classical concept of General Nature and the Universal.

The Trustees of the Victoria and Albert Museum

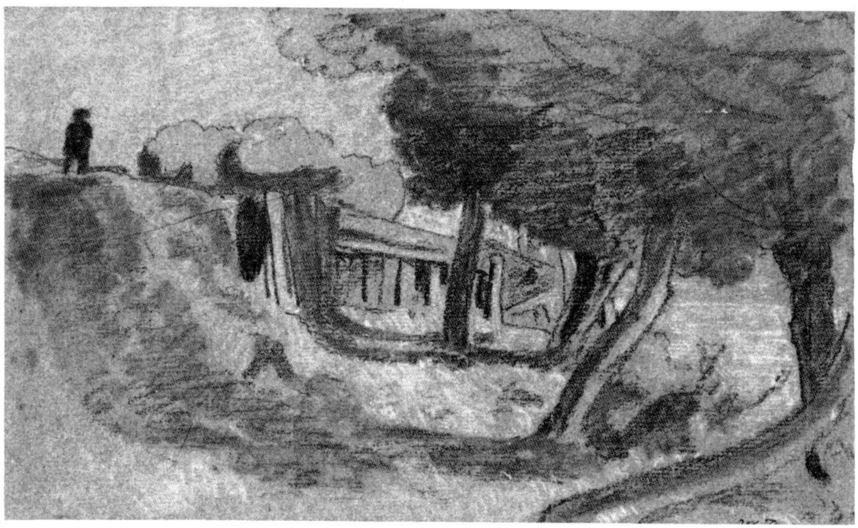

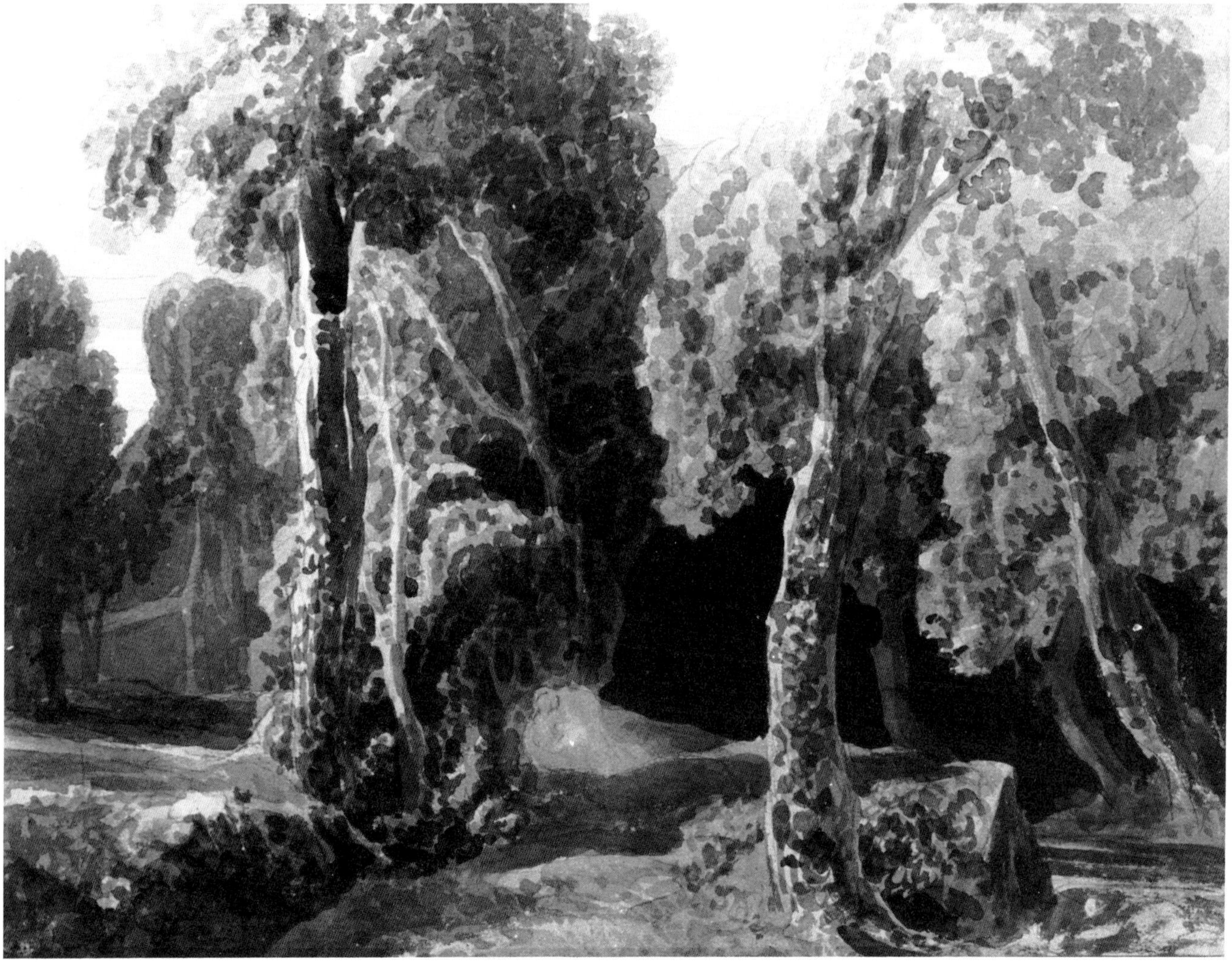

8 Sketching Society subject

datable 1808
Pencil and brown monochrome wash on cream wove
27 × 34.8

Prov: Christie's 21 November 1978 Lot 1 (part), bought Abbot and Holder.

Turner was among those artists involved in the third phase of the Sketching Society, founded in 1808 by J.J. Chalon and Francis Stevens. Correctly entitled *The Society for Epic and Pastoral Design*, it became known as Chalon's Society. A minute-book of the Society records Turner as having attended only thirteen of the weekly meetings. Subjects for illustrations were chosen from the poets both ancient and modern. The third season (1809–10) took seven quotations from James Thompson's *The Seasons*; the fourth, five subjects from Homer's *Odyssey*, the fifth, seven from Walter Scott's *Lady of the Lake*. The neglect of the figures in the present drawing means, of course, that the subject is not discoverable. Yet the theme of figures resting beside a stream beneath a dense cover of foliage would seem to indicate less a traceable line of poetry, than a general Retirement subject.

Private Collection

9 A view of Waddon Wood in the village of Waddington near Clitheroe in the county of Lancaster

1808
Pencil and watercolour on white wove, cut, sponged and abraded, all but the margins badly faded.
45.8 × 64.8
Signed and dated *W. Turner 1808*, signed and inscribed with title verso

Prov: T.L. Parker, 1808; R.E.S. Willison; Agnew's.
Ref: Hardie, p.235.

The view may be that from Browsholme Moor looking across to, on the right, Beacon Hill, and on the left Easington Fell. The village of Waddington is seen brightly illuminated in the middle distance at the far right. The picture was not exhibited; most likely it was a commission from Thomas Lister Parker, a patron of, among others, J.M.W. Turner, who was later to buy the present artist's *View from King's Weston Down, near Bristol* at the SPW exhibition of 1810. The Parker family seat is Browsholme Hall which stands about a mile away from the site of this picture and two miles from Whitewell, the subject of another major watercolour issuing from this trip (Christie's, 10 July 1984, lot 126; Hardie's identification of *Waddon Wood* as the work bought by Samuel Naylor and now in the Huntington Library seems to be due to a confusion on his part). Ostensibly, *Waddon* is accurate topographically, though we may be led to question this by the obvious similarities the foreground displays to such pictures as *Scene near Woodstock* (Cat.13). Both drawings show a river at the extreme lower right, and though placed differently, Turner contrives to include in both a cottage partly obscured by the ground it seems to nestle into. The allusion, quite clearly, is to the organic rubric proposed by the Picturesque, and it neatly demonstrates how an artist working within the confines of the naturalist idiom may still speak efficiently and compellingly of subjects that are strictly external to the literal meaning of the image.

Martyn Gregory

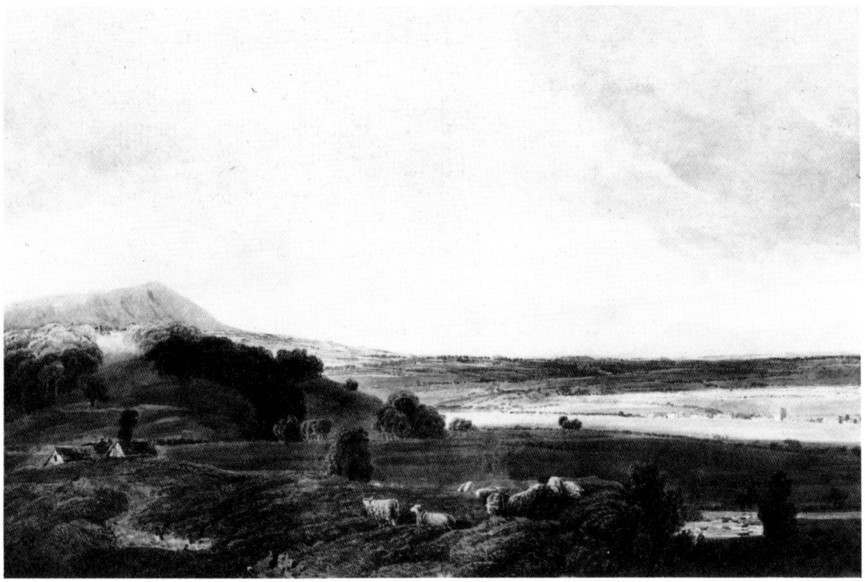

10 Sketchbook

(c.1803–c.1808)
White wove, watermarked, 1794; leather bound, double clasp.
22 drawings hard pencil, 14 soft pencil, 1 pen and ink
22.8 × 29.2 (page size)
Inscribed in pencil in another hand on inside cover: *Sketchbook of William Turner of Oxford*; individual pages inscribed with topographical location of drawing

The book has been used at two distinct times. It was thought that the group of hard pencil drawings documented an early tour through Wales. However, the evidence of a series of identical drawings by William Delamotte (VAM album 95.G.53) dated 1803 would now seem to suggest that Turner copied Delamotte's originals, probably before leaving Oxford to join

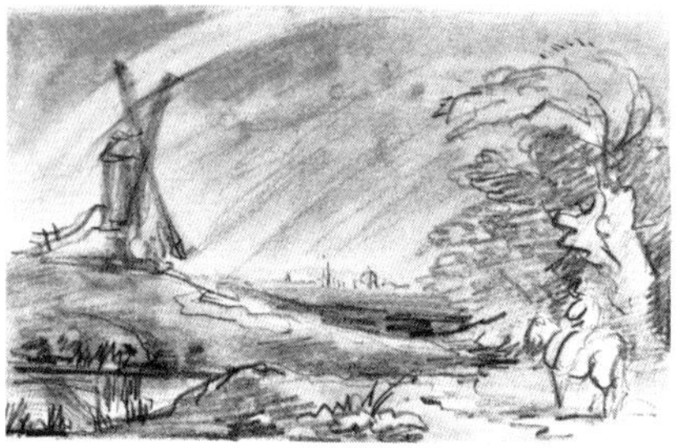

Varley in 1804. The date would account for the juvenile handling and the weak perspective evident in this group. The fourteen drawings in soft pencil may well be aides-memoires for finished oils or watercolours. One can be identified as a view of Waddington and is clearly related to Cat. 9.

There are also two ink portraits that are strongly reminiscent of Varley's Zodiacal Heads.

The drawing shown here, depicting a windmill and rider, has obvious affinities with later compositions, but cannot be related to any specific work. The boldly managed chiaroscuro of the sky and rainbow is technically more advanced than the hard pencil group, and, with the evidence of the Waddington drawing, would suggest a date of c.1807–8.

Private Collection

11 Estuary with figure on horseback

(c.1808–12)
Oil on thick card
15.3 × 16

The broad and individually somewhat homogenous areas of colour would suggest a date in the region of 1805–10. (The traditional title of *Head of a Loch* has no apparent foundation.) This date is supported by a related wash drawing from an album now in the Huntington Library. This album contains drawings that date variously from c.1805 to c.1815. That related to the present picture (71.1A.1) shows the oil to be a compression of a much wider composition. The configuration of figures and cattle seen against a high bank of cloud recalls Cuyp. For his example in the faithful rendering of natural light, which was seen to ennoble his mean subject-matter, Cuyp was enormously influential at this date. In 1821, a watercolour of Turner's was remarked on as "a fine example of light and breadth, and the repose equal to that of Cuyp" (*Literary Gazette*, 12 May 1821, p.297).

Private Collection

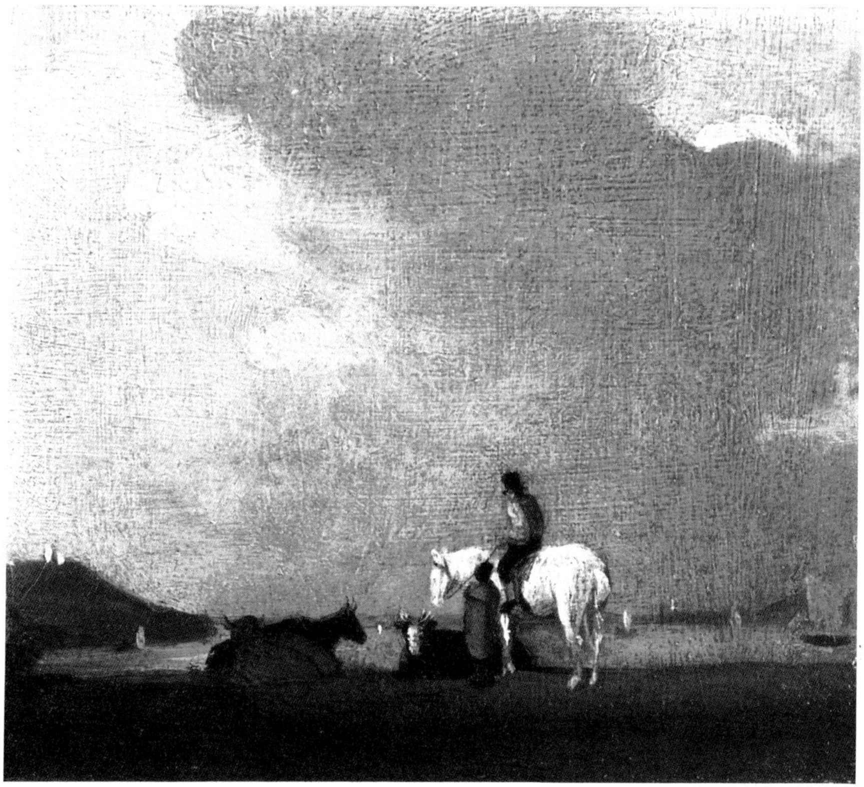

12 Durdham Down with a knight on horseback

(c.1808)
Pencil and sepia wash on heavy cream laid
21.3 × 16.5
Inscribed verso *Durdham Down* together with two anatomical studies in pen and ink

Prov: Lady Donnelly, by whom presented, 1902 (VAM D.336-1902).

Formerly known as *The Joust*, although the visual evidence is against such a title. The rider does not confront an opponent, rather, he seems to lead a group of horsemen from the right. The view they burst into looks across the River Avon from above St Vincent's Rocks near Clifton; this was considered one of the great English beauty-spots and occurs several times in the Huntington albums (as does the rider, though in another context), in drawings all datable to c.1808–9. The knight is drawn directly from an etching after Claude's *Liber Veritatis* of *St George Killing the Dragon*. Given the events of the Continental war, it does not seem far-fetched to see the drawing as a patriotic statement, proclaiming the combined strength of English scenery and the English character.

The Trustees of the Victoria and Albert Museum, London

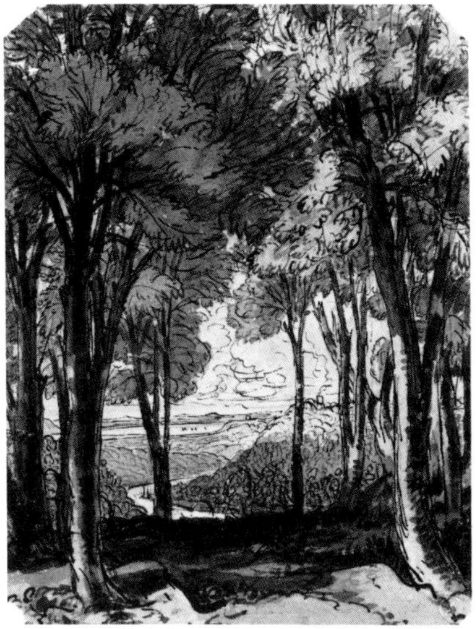

13 Scene near Woodstock

1809
Watercolour on cream wove, cut abraded and sponged
56.5 × 74.5
Signed verso, *W. Turner of Oxford* and inscribed *Mr. Swinburne*

Prov: E. Swinburne, 1809; Rev. E.P. Baker, FSA; The Society of Antiquaries; Sotheby's, 19 November 1981, lot 192.
Exh: SPW 1908 (110), £21.

Although long known as *Otmoor*, this magisterial watercolour has recently been identified as the work exhibited in 1809 as *Scene near Woodstock*. The view is taken from the side of the Oxford to Banbury road about one mile from Shipton-on-Cherwell, looking towards the North-East. The bridge over the Cherwell at Enslow is just visible on the right, below the steep incline now known as 'Gibraltar Rock'. Turner's attention to the detail of the scene extends to the depiction of the stark limey earth visible in the ruts of the main road bearing the rider, beneath the shallow top-soil. With this work, Turner has liberated himself at a single stroke from the topographical watercolour tradition. The title is inexplicit as to location, and the eye looks in vain for any landmark which might lend significance to what is so patently an actual view. The wheeling birds, the straining trees and the rider's flapping cloak all emphasise the force of the wind, which drives the clouds into a powerful diagonal, countered by that of the churned earth in the foreground. Everything is in a state of flux; the cult of transience at the core of the Picturesque is pushed to new expressive limits, as the all-but-anonymous landscape and the anonymous rider have no response to make to the viewer's demand for the sense of it all, other than their too-obvious vulnerability to the forces acting on them.

The scale of Turner's achievement in the richly suggestive language derived from such an unpromising vocabulary is hardly less than that of Wordsworth, who in Hazlitt's words, "like Rembrandt, has a faculty of making something out of nothing, that is out of himself, by the medium through which he sees and with which he clothes the barrenest subject".

Reproduced in colour

Private Collection

14 Whichwood Forest, Oxfordshire

1809
Watercolour with touches of bodycolour on heavy cream wove, cut, sponged and extensively gummed
60.7 × 79.3
Signed recto *W. Turner Shipton on Cher. Oxon.*; inscribed verso *Scene near where a pleasure fair was formerly held in Whichwood Forest, Oxfordshire, William Turner, Shipton on Cherwell, Oxon. 1809*

Prov: J. Fulleylove, 1901; A.T. Hollingsworth; his sale, Christie's, 19 April 1929, lot 82, bought Agnew's on behalf of the Museum (VAM P.136-1929).
Exh: SPW 1809 (243), 20 guineas; Fine Art Society, *The Watercolour Art of the Nineteenth Century*, January 1901 (20) *Wooded Landscape near Oxford*.
Ref: *Artwork*, Vol. VI, Spring 1930, p.48 & 53, repr. p.52; C. Johnson, *English Painting*, 1932, p.207, repr. pl.29; Hardie, p.235, repr. pl.229; Herrmann, p.242.

Wychwood Forest is only a few miles from the corner of western Oxfordshire where Turner was born, and he probably knew it well from his earliest years. Certainly the works depicting the forest suggest that it aroused the strongest feelings in the artist. A horse-fair and a pleasure fair were held annually in the forest, a tradition opposed by the Duke of Marlborough, the Forest Ranger. In 1857 he managed to abolish these festivities on a permanent basis but it is evident that in 1808 he had some success in excluding the caravans and sideshows, despite the rights of common enjoyed by the surrounding parishes. It can be surmised that Turner was particularly provoked by the disruptions to the tradition, for not only did he inscribe the reverse of the picture but noted again in his copy of the 1808 SPW exhibition catalogue "near where the fair was held". Given these circumstances, the site could be understood as an appropriate scene for an elegiac musing on the passing of a local custom. The subject of the forest interior was traditionally linked with the concept of Retirement, and Turner may have been developing this theme. That he was familiar with this notion of withdrawal from Society to enjoy mediative communion with Nature is evident from an early drawing (see fig.3). In Alison, the idea was taken further and inactive Retirement proposed as the state in which the most fruitful creative and aesthetic insights could be engendered, and this watercolour may offer a demonstration of the transforming power of the imagination.

The conventional melancholy figures associated with the depiction of the concept of Retirement are missing and there is none of that sense of tranquillity that might be expected; the writhing trees and the calling horse create a particularly turbulent effect. Turner's first hand experience of the forest is mediated by his knowledge of Titian's *St Peter Martyr*, at the time generally considered the outstanding example of "serious" landscape. He has appropriated the overall organisation and atmosphere of the work, and many of the individual details. The central struggling figures of the saint and his assassin have been translated into a pair of trees, which spring from the same root and seem to anthropomorphise, the left-hand tree apparently recoiling from that on the right. Some act of violence is thus suggested, which seems appropriate in the context of the contemporary threats to enclose the forest (see Arthur Young, *General View of the Agriculture of Oxfordshire, 1809*) and the Duke of Marlborough's opposition to the forest fair. It is conceivable that, for Turner, this painting had special connotations, representing the imposition of authority over local tradition.

However turbulent his representation of the forest itself, our appreciation of its nature is considerably heightened by the glimpse of a different scenery to the right, an escape route which the eye siezes on as a release from the dark confines of the trees, The impact of this vista relies on the contrast of technique, as well as subject-matter. Where the treatment of the forest presents a virtuoso demonstration of the mixed handling available to the ambitious watercolourist, the open ground and sky are rendered with exceptional purity in large flat areas of colour. Hardie's comparison of this area of the work with Cotman is irresistible, but the great appeal of *Whichwood Forest* does not depend purely on technical or formal excellence; it is in the balancing of so many components that the work achieves its unique intensity, dark with light, complicated, crowded space with emptiness, private emotion with the aspiration and upheaval of the romantic spirit.

Reproduced in colour

The Trustees of the Victoria and Albert Museum

15 The South door at Quenington, Gloucestershire

(c.1810)
Watercolour on heavy cream wove, cut and sponged, laid down on to card
28.9 × 49.5
Inscribed on Vokins frame:
Painted by Turner/for Leopold Redpath/ bought at his sale.

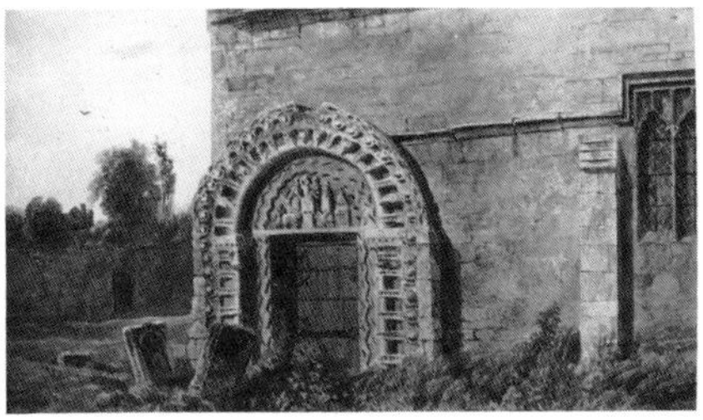

Prov: Leopold Redpath; his sale, Christie's, 23 May 1857, lot 284 (J.M.W. Turner, *A Church with an ancient Norman porch*), 11 guineas to A. Gardner.

Turner exhibited two views of the doors at Quenington at the Watercolour Society; the first in 1810: *A Saxon Door at Quinnington, Gloucestershire* (sold Rev. G. Johnson) and the following year another, *North Door at Quinnington Church, Gloucestershire* (sold Mr Lowry). Stylistically, the present version must date from the same time. There is a watercolour of the Romanesque West door of Iffley church identical in format (Bodleian Library, Ms.Top. Oxon. a.21. fol. 18) and, on a similar theme, a representation of the porch of the fourteenth-century church at Shipton was exhibited in 1808.

The simple frontal view is a response to the priority placed by the antiquarian on information above imaginative flair. The popularity of the subject may be seen as part of the growing interest in the aesthetic qualities of early medieval art, its rugged simplicity being increasingly appreciated for its lack of sophistication and "manner".

Private Collection

16 Oxford from Hinksey Hill

1810
Pencil, watercolour and touches of bodycolour on cream wove
26.2 × 39.7
Signed and dated *W. Turner 1810*

Prov: Purchased, 1931.
Ref: Herrmann, p.242, repr. p.243.

The device of a figure seen from behind and standing passively before a landscape, assumes great importance in later nineteenth-century German and American painting, where it is used primarily as an emblem of contemplative union. Turner's landscapes at this date do not exhibit the visionary quality found in Caspar David Friedrich or, considerably later, in Asher Brown Durand. By giving this figure a larger scale than that of conventional staffage, and by emphasising his inactivity in the hands-behind-the-back stance, Turner succeeds in chanelling our perception of the scene through the figure, who thus acts as a surrogate.

There is a related print (Cat.28).

The Visitors of the Ashmolean Museum, Oxford

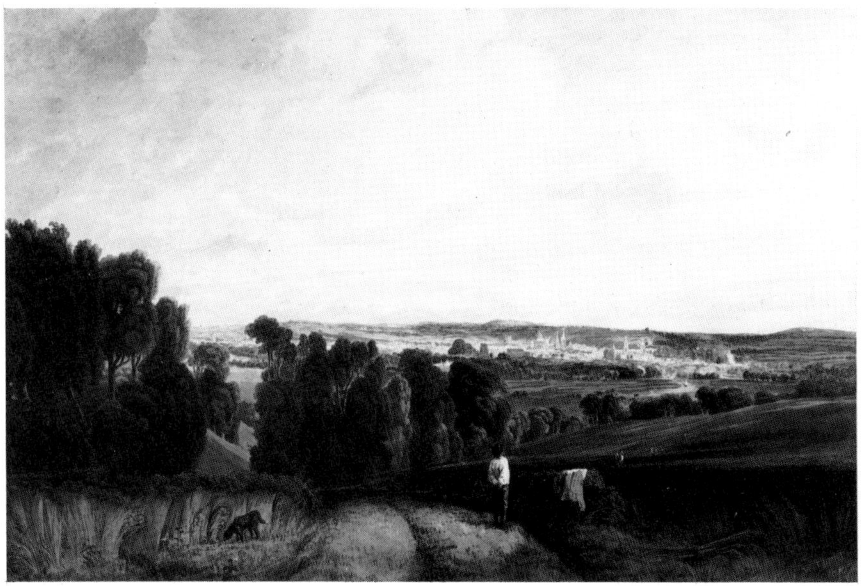

17 The Glebe Corn

(c.1810–12?)
Oil on canvas
33 × 48
Signed and numbered on the stretcher: *No.2 Wm. Turner Oxford*

Prov: L.R. Phelps, Provost of Oriel College, Oxford; his sale, Provost's Lodge, 2 October 1929, lot 122 (*Harvest Scene*).

The image of a landowner in close touch with both his land and with his labourers and their families had obvious importance for Turner. Here he varies his more usual hierarchical structure of the gentleman-farmer on horseback paternally overseeing his inferiors, and instead depicts the owner assessing the quality of the corn.

R.E. Alton, MC

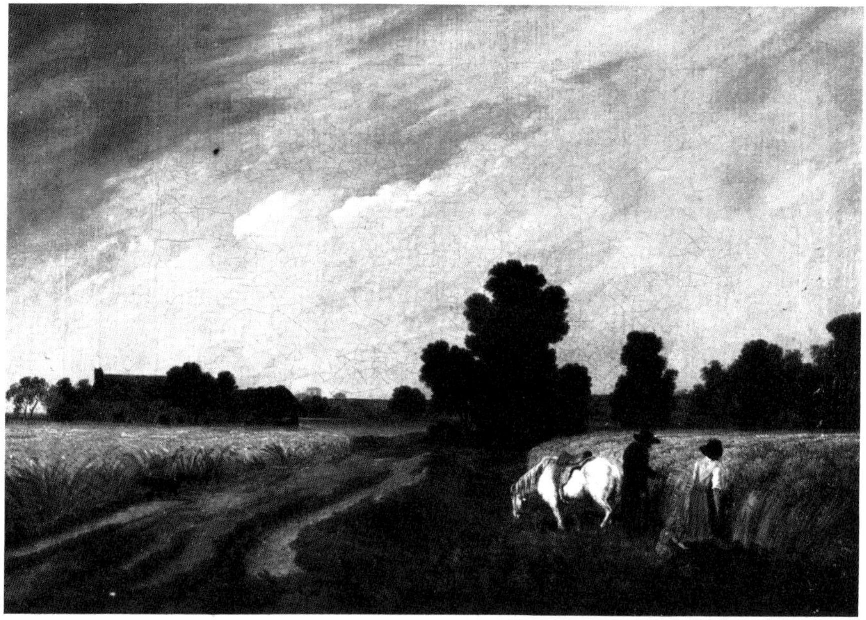

18 View from a Salt Marsh near Shirehampton, Gloucestershire

(c.1811)
Watercolour and bodycolour on heavy cream wove, cut, sponged, abraded and gummed
34 × 76
Inscribed with title verso

Prov: Herbert Powell; Lady Powell bequest 1968 (VAM P.48-1968).

The Shirehampton Marshes at the mouth of the River Avon provided Turner with the almost featureless expanse that he particularly favoured. He uses the formal strategy deployed in *Scene near Woodstock* (Cat.13) in which the rigid division of the paper by an almost straight horizon is punctured by one or two verticals that have little visual weight, but nonetheless assume a central determining role in the picture simply by virtue of being the only objects on which the eye can seize. As in *Oxford from Hinksey* (Cat.16) the figure seen from behind acts in some ways as a surrogate presence for the viewer, but the image of the passive figure seems also to have been Turner's observation and acknowledgment of the concept of nature as divine curriculum, the passage through which would inevitably lead to moral perfection.

The exploitation of the tension between opposing thematic elements, fundamental to Dutch landscape painting of the seventeenth century, was taken up most fruitfully by Gainsborough in the eighteenth century. There is evidence of Turner's interest in the Dutch elements of Gainsborough's work in his pen and wash copy of the *Panoramic Landscape* (Collection Duke of Norfolk, Hayes Cat.50) preserved in the Huntington Albums (see introduction to section 1 p.25), where Gainsborough has opposed a windmill, dependent on the flow of the elements, and a rugged tree-stump, an image of resolute immobility before those elements. *Shirehampton* appropriates the same structure: in the contrast of the statuesque figure with the scudding yacht, the shepherd attains the simple stoical dependability and dignity admired at this time.

Reproduced in colour

The Trustees of the Victoria and Albert Museum

2. 1812–1823

It is not known if Turner was based in London after 1810. In 1810 he gives his address simply as "at Woodstock", and this may indicate that he initially returned to live at Shipton Manor. For the following three years he gives his address as "at Mr Passands High St Oxford" and his business address as Varley's in London. In 1816 he was "At Mr Delamotte's near Oxford".

In 1812, under the pressure of declining attendance figures, the Watercolour Society suffered a collapse, and while it was immediately resuscitated by those who were willing to admit oils, receipts had fallen sharply and it is evident that London was no longer able to support so large a community of water-colourists. Even so well-established a figure as Havell was induced by the unfavourable climate to accept an invitation to travel as a draughtsman with Lord Amherst's embassy to China in 1815; in the same year, David Cox, by then also a successful, if less ambitious, landscape painter took a position as a drawing master at a girls' school in Hereford. Given these circumstances it is perhaps not so surprising that Turner, despite his early acclaim, should choose to establish himself in Oxford.

The work exhibited at the Royal Academy and the Watercolour Society between 1807 and 1811 was all drawn from Oxfordshire or the neighbouring counties, and it is consistent with the general thrust of his doctrinal sympathies that this should be so. His profound commitment to the empirically known, and his resultant affiliation with the emergent Naturalist aesthetic in its emphasis on the power of thorough and deep knowledge of a subject to transform poetically a common scene, makes such a return seem almost inevitable. Here there are important similarities to Constable's attachment to his native Dedham and with that artist's belief that, through his unique power to mediate the material the locality produced, the small area around his father's fields and mills was sufficient as the subjects of ambitious art. The point was not lost on contemporary observers who attributed Turner's "truth of nature to his observations upon the ever changing effects on such scenery during his residence in the country the greater part of the year". (*Ackerman's Repository* on *View from Dowdeswell* SPW 1812 (86)). However much this may have impressed one critic, it is still possible to argue that the move to Oxford eventually resulted in his gradual decline in the eyes of his contemporaries to the position of provincial drawing-master.

Turner is said to have had a great many pupils in Oxford, although none ever rose to any eminence as watercolourists. Although there was little general interest in the visual arts among the University population, a number of undergraduates took lessons, and other pupils were presumably supplied from the wealthier townsfolk. Considering the population of Oxford, it is perhaps surprising to find Turner had almost no competion for his practice. Following Delamotte, Hugh O'Neill was active as a drawing master for a few years before leaving for Bristol in around 1812. Not until the trade directories of the late 1820s do we have any evidence of the strength of the competition, figures fluctuate, but each edition lists only one or two "Professors of Drawing", apart from the handful of "Artists". In the mid-century the best-established such

"Professor" was Joseph Vickers Richardson, some of whose rather perfunctory work survives among the topographical collections of the Bodleian Library. Interestingly, Turner never appears in the directories in the category of "Professor of Drawing" and is always noted under "Artist", thus indicating his true area of commitment. However, in his response to the census of 1851 he called himself "Artist & Teacher of Landscape Painting".

Turner's attachment to Oxford did not preclude a vigorous programme of summer touring during the 1810s and 1820s. Purely on the evidence of exhibited work, he seems to have made a trip to the Lake District in 1814; in 1817 he toured Central and North Wales, and a number of dated sketches survive, as they do for a trip to the Peak District in 1818. The smaller watercolours from these years present a conventional Varleyian Picturesque. The true development of his talent, as represented in ambitious exhibition pieces, is much harder to assess. On the one hand, work for the local market probably gave rise to the increasing number of small, rather unsatisfying views; a set of etchings of Oxford subjects produced in 1816 or 1817 (Cat. 25–28) may never have been published, but further attests to his efforts to attract local clients. On the other hand, the majority of exhibited oils, and many watercolours were destroyed, amounting to almost half his total in 1815 and 1817. There is a complete absence of finished, dated work for the entire period before *Pope's Tower, the Old Kitchen, etc, Stanton Harcourt, Oxfordshire* in 1822 (Cat.42), although the *Vale of Ffestiniog* (Cat.31), tentatively attributed on the basis of a putative stylistic continuity to 1817, shows no decline in his powers. The style that emerges in the 1820s is a mellow, considered one, less exuberant than much of the early work, demonstrating Turner's restraint in his attachment to the subject matter.

19 Portmeadow, Oxford

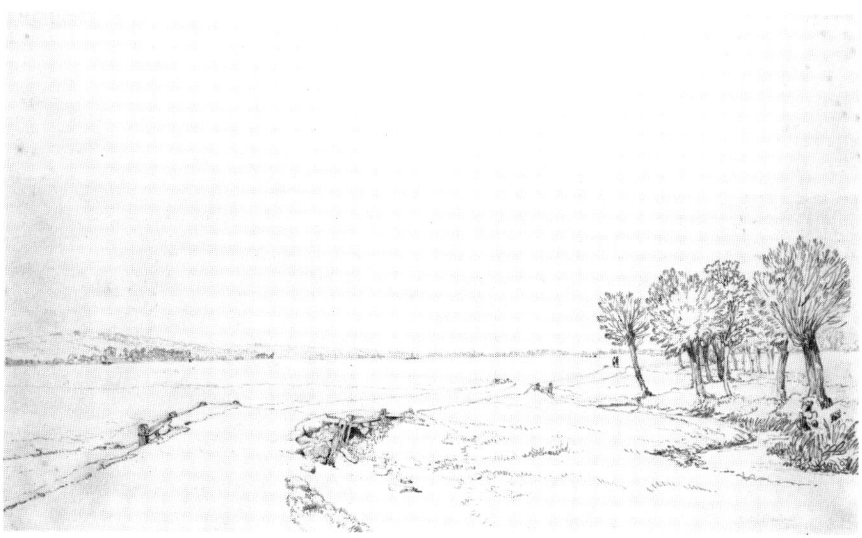

(c.1812?)
Pencil on cream wove
15.9 × 47
Signed and inscribed *Portmeadow. W. Turner*

Prov: L.R. Phelps, Provost of Oriel College, Oxford; S.D. Kitson, by whom bequeathed, 1939 (VAM E.204-1939).

Turner seems to have been particularly fascinated by the contrast obtained in the depiction of a largely empty and featureless expanse in which float patches of high resolution pencil work. Here the incident is pushed into the narrow strip of the horizon or confined to the immediate foreground, and it does not seem too impressionistic to sense the delight with which the "hungry" eye seizes upon such areas as, for example, the constellation of marks and lines that compose the small bridge.

The Trustees of the Victoria and Albert Museum

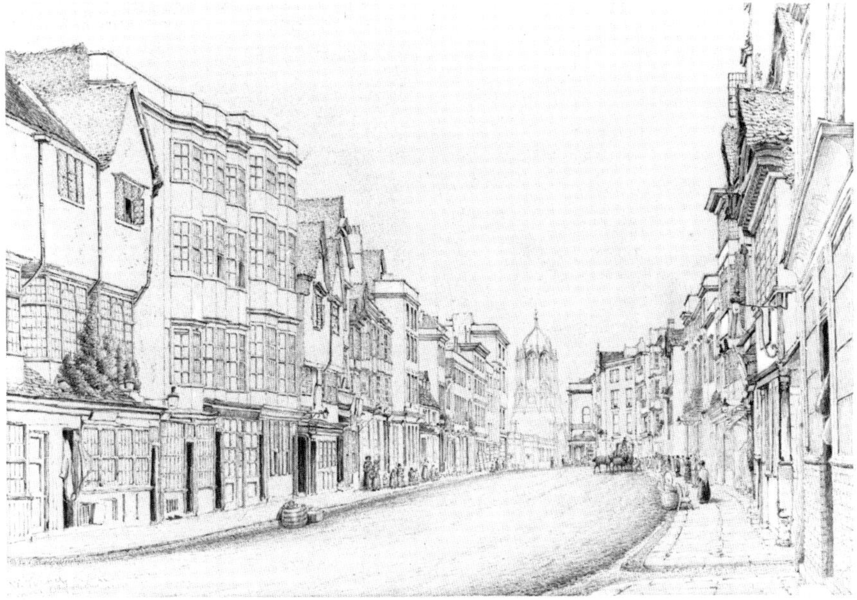

20 Cornmarket

(after 1812)
Pencil, heightened with white bodycolour (now discoloured) on cream, possibly prepared, wove
24.8 × 36.3
Signed *W. Turner Oxford*, inscribed on old mount: *The Cornmarket Street as it appeared in the year 1812*

Prov: Mrs E.T. Leeds, by whom presented, 1957.
Ref: Herrmann, p.245, repr. p.246.

In later life, Turner produced many topographical drawings based on earlier studies, and the evidence suggests he replicated his originals quite consciencously. It is not possible to say whether this drawing dates from 1812 or considerably later. The exceptional detail suggests it may have been made with some specific project in mind, possibly Ackermann's *University of Oxford* of 1814. The hard, clean pencil work shows Turner's prowess as an architectural draughtsman. He seems to have been at pains to surrender his individual "hand" to the subject with the same passivity as that produced in work made with the camera obscura. Another, less-finished, version of this drawing was reproduced on the Oxford Almanack of 1919.

The Visitors of the Ashmolean Museum, Oxford

21 View of Oxford, from the Gallery in the Observatory

1814
Etching and aquatint, hand-coloured in watercolour, the foreground foliage heavily gummed. Slightly marked by offsetting
Plate 25.3 × 29.9 Image 21 × 28.3
Signed on plate *W. Turner delt.*
J. Bluck sculpt, inscribed with title and dated, *Published July 1st 1814*

This print forms the frontispiece to Ackermann's *A History of the University of Oxford its Colleges, Halls and Public Buildings* (Vol.II). Although Turner's drawing was given the prominence of the frontispiece, there was no other work of his reproduced in the volumes. There is a pencil sketch (c.1807) in an album in the Ashmolean Museum, Oxford, which shows a similar interest in the Oxford skyline seen under a dramatic "effect". Here, in the strongly directional lighting, the straining trees and sharply deflected smoke streaming from the chimneys of the city, Turner demonstrates his ability to transform poetically a straightforward view into one of considerable emotional power.

Mr Christopher Titterington

22 Composition

(c.1813)
Pencil and white bodycolour on blue-grey wove cartridge
18.2 × 26.5
Dated on cover of original album:
1813

Prov: Thomas Penrose, New College, Oxford, 1814, 6 guineas (album); Lawrence of Crewkerne, 22 November 1979, lot 1; Agnew's.

This, and the following drawing, are both from an album acquired by Thomas Penrose in 1814. Penrose was a fellow of New College from 1788 until 1815, when he left Oxford to become vicar of Writtle-cum-Roxwell, Essex, a living he occupied until his death in 1851. It seems likely that the album was acquired as a memento of Oxford days, although not all the drawings are of Oxford subjects. The album contained twenty-four drawings in all which show the considerable scope of Turner's practice at this date. Replicas exist in pencil of two of the drawings. Further, two appear again in pencil and wash in the Huntington albums, two are known in oils and four in full watercolour. Two were used for the set of etchings issued by Turner in 1816 or 1817 (Cat.26 and Cat.28) and one engraved by G. Hollar for R. Pearson's *Walks in Oxford*, published in Oxford in 1817.

This drawing is unusual for Turner in as much as it is an invention composed from a number of studies or possibly fabricated by the artist. The idiom is much more common in John Varley, particularly after around 1808.

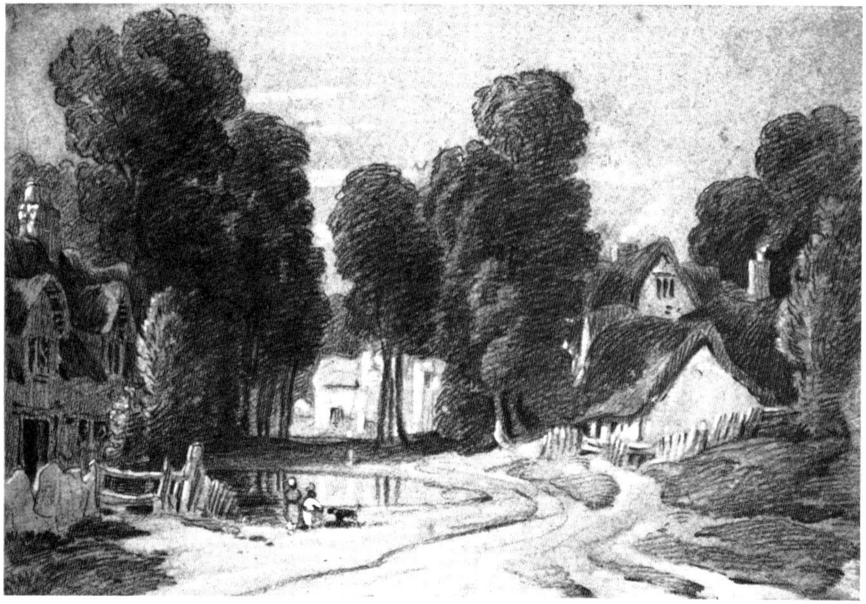

Cat.22

Cat.23

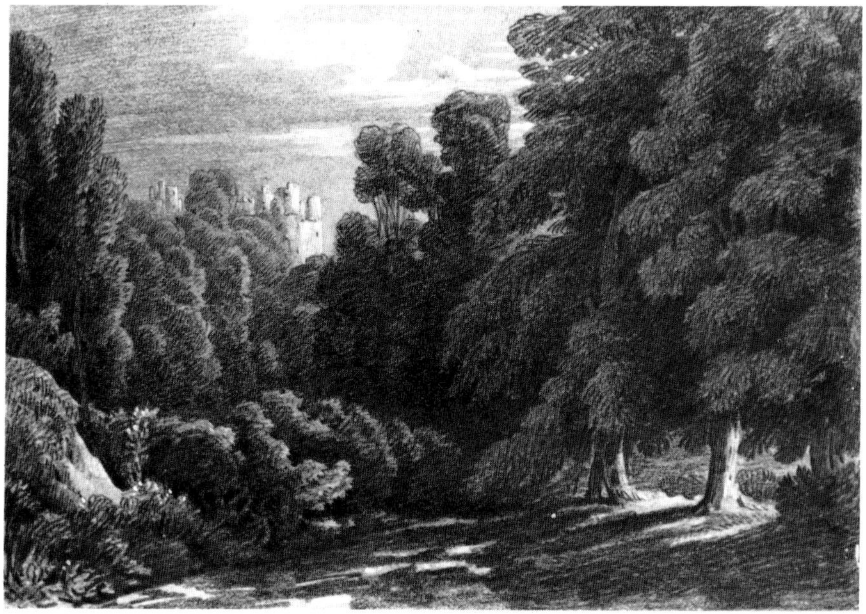

The village was seen as the ideal nucleus of the Picturesque community, and here Turner depicts exactly those features that were most admired. We have the sense that its apparently careless layout is, in fact, a response to the specific needs of its inhabitants in fine balance with the demands of the landscape itself.

Mr A.J. Bergman

23 Goodrich Castle

(c.1813)
Pencil and touches of white bodycolour on blue-grey wove cartridge
18.2 × 26.5
Dated on cover of original album: *1813*

Prov: See Cat. 22.

Another drawing from the album acquired by Thomas Penrose in 1814.

Turner seems to have made a tour of the Wye valley by at least 1809. Several pencil and wash drawings from the Huntington albums show him to have been experimenting with the transforming properties of twilight or lurid storm effects often realised over identical subjects. There is a version of this picture in the Huntington albums; for once the powerful castle walls induced Turner to cloak the whole in a powerful chiaroscuro in both cases.

Mr & Mrs John Goodfellow

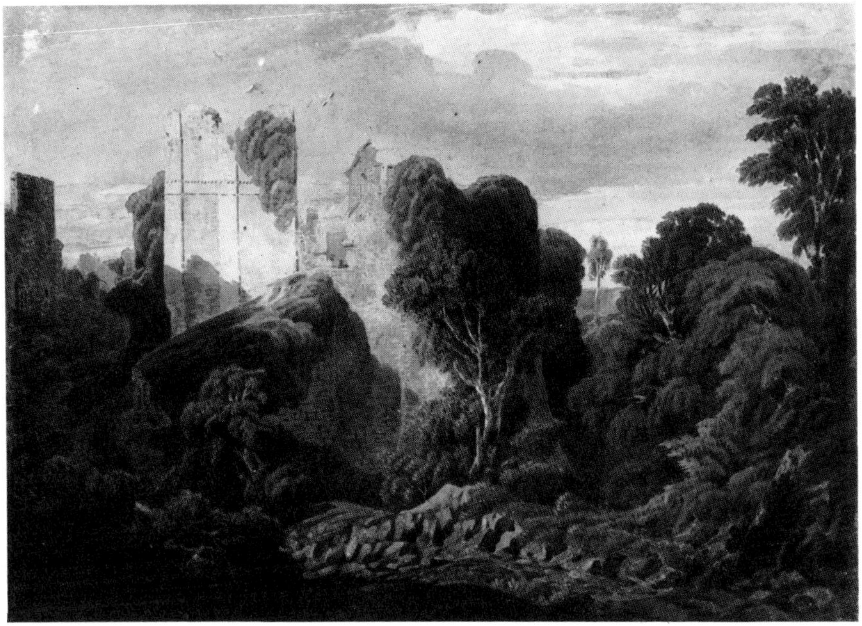

24 Raglan Castle

(c.1813–16)
Pencil, watercolour and bodycolour on cream wove
29.7 × 41.5

Prov: Purchased, 1867.
Ref: Hardie, pl.231.

Raglan relates quite closely to the drawing of the same subject in the Penrose album of 1814 (see Cat.22).

Nature here seems arrested in the act of claiming back the remains of the castle; the ground seems to bulge and the foliage to writhe as they lay claim to material that was once wholly theirs. The jagged and angular blocks of broken earth that form the edge of the foreground path are perhaps some of the earliest manifestations of the invention that was to grace his foregrounds from now onwards. This is the clue to the curiously animated forms that surround the fabric of the castle, for only the architecture itself can be based on pre-recorded information; the lip of the picture and the vegetation are playful inventions, animations that seem almost to parody the doctrinal requirements of the Picturesque. Such a capricious treatment of form brings to mind the Rococo underpinning of Gainsborough's practice of inventing landscapes on the kitchen table from pieces of brocoli and coal.

The Trustees of the British Museum

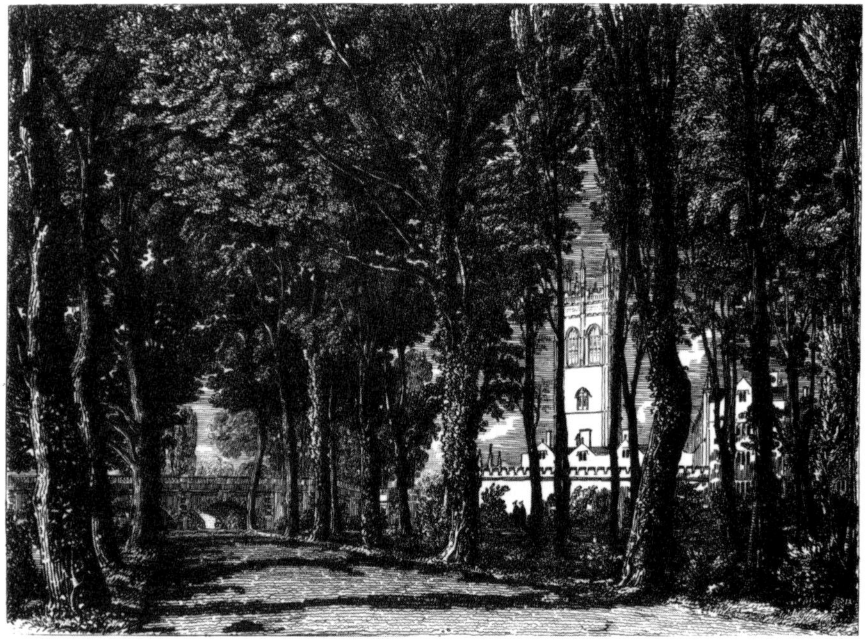

25 Magdalen Water Walk

(Set dates to 1816–17)
Etching on cream wove
Plate 16.2 × 21.6 Image 12.9 × 18

One of a set of seven views around Oxford. With Cat.26 to 28, the remaining subjects are *The City Wall*, *View of Oxford from Binsey*, and *New Gardens, New College*. There is a complete set in the Victoria and Albert Museum including a working proof of *Oxford Castle*, and a set in the British Museum, both before letters. The present subject has been extensively rebitten and details such as the dons walking beneath the trees considerably emphasised. The set is traditionally dated c.1816–17, an estimate reinforced by the close similarity in the treatment of this subject to a pair of drawings of *Balliol College Grove in the year 1816* (later replicas; Balliol College, Oxford). In terms of technique and scale, they relate closely to William Delamotte's *Twenty Etchings* (Sandhurst, 1816), which were drawn, etched and published by the artist. In the SPW catalogues Turner gives his address in 1816 as "at Mr. Delamotte's, near Oxford", and it is perhaps to the example of Delamotte's commercial venture that this set by Turner owes its origin. The similarities make it probable that Turner at least took advice from Delamotte, and perhaps even used the same printing facilities.

The Trustees of the British Museum
(with Cat.26–28)

26 Folly Bridge

Etching on cream wove
Plate 17.8 × 21.7 Image 11.7 × 18.7

One of the best known of all Oxford landmarks, there are similar views by many of Turner's contemporaries.

27 St Giles

(c.1816–17)
Etching on cream wove
Plate 16.4 × 21.7 Image 12.7 × 18.9

The view is the same as in a pencil and wash drawing dated 1820 (Cat.38). A later watercolour based on this print was reproduced on the Oxford Almanack for 1896.

28 View of Oxford from Hinksey

(c.1816–17)
Etching on cream wove
Plate 16.5 × 21.7 Image 10.7 × 18.9

A popular view based on the watercolour of 1810 (Cat.16), of which a drawing also appeared in the Penrose album (see Cat.22).

29 Meadows in flood

(c.1816–20)
Sepia wash on grey-brown wove
27.6 × 44
Prov: L.R. Phelps, Provost of Oriel College, Oxford; S.D. Kitson by whom bequeathed, 1939 (VAM E.201-1939).

The scene is just after sunset, and the afterglow on the distant horizon is reflected on to the surface of the shallow pools of flood-water. Through the dimly lit woods are visible cattle and figures, though the "driving home the flock" theme is lost in the magnificence of the evening "effect". This Turner achieves simply by brush and varying strengths of a single wash.

The Trustees of the Victoria and Albert Museum

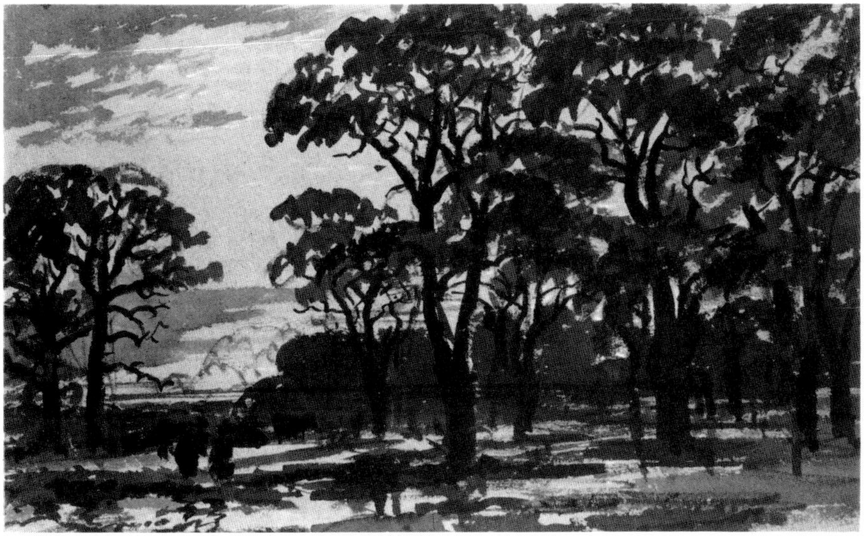

Cat.29

30 Wooded landscape

(c.1816–20)
Oil on millboard
22 × 29

Prov: F.F. Madan, by whom presented, 1939.
Ref: Herrmann, p.246.

Turner manages to evoke a considerable sense of scale. This is achieved mainly in the strong perspectival view of the voluminous and massive clouds. These penetrate the curtain established by the trees that run parallel to the plane of vision and seem in the top right corner to extend out almost above our heads.

Throughout his life Turner seems to have been fascinated by positive/negative spatial effects. This can be seen here in the line of individually articulated tree trunks at centre right. This interest can clearly be seen, for instance, in the early *Scene near Woodstock* (Cat.13).

The Visitors of the Ashmolean Museum, Oxford

31 The Vale of Ffestiniog

(c.1817)
Watercolour and bodycolour on cream wove, scraped, cut, sponged and extensively gummed
57.1 × 88.9

Prov: R. Nesham; his sale, Christie's, 30 July 1924, lot 90, 14 guineas, bought Palser; A.E. Anderson, by whom presented, 1925.

The "effect" looks to be that of a storm clearing off and the brilliant handling of the chiaroscuro of the interacting cloud and mountains is not unlike those watercolours produced in the area by Cotman and Munn on their tour of 1807. This drawing's firm handling and deft subtractive highlights, particularly those employed in the fern, clearly relate to the handling

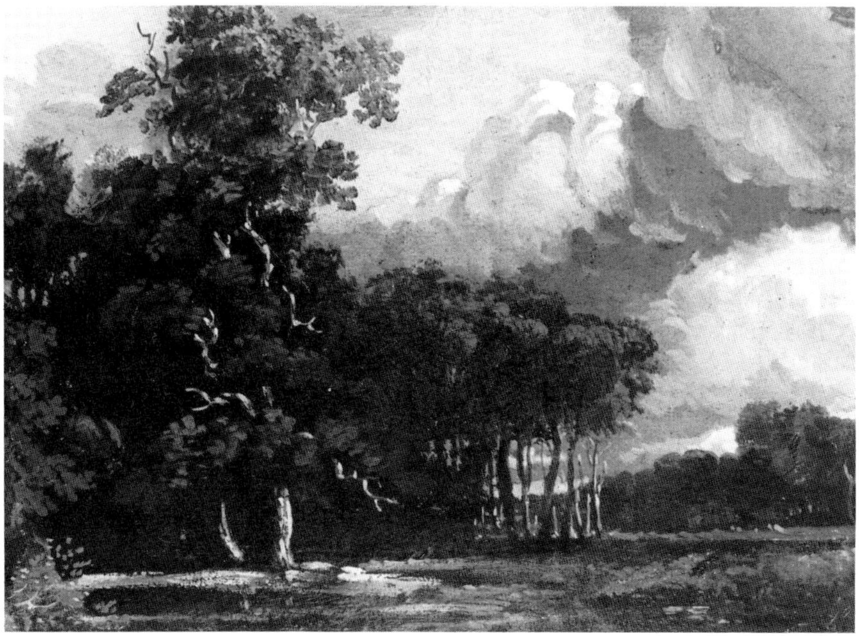

of such highlights in *Raglan Castle* (Cat.24). Here, however, the darks are heavily gummed in order to give depth of tone. The sentimental pose struck by the two ponies is an eighteenth-century convention used frequently by Stubbs, Sawrey Gilpin and occasionally Gainsborough.

Reproduced in colour

The Visitors of the Ashmolean Museum, Oxford

32 Conwy Castle

(c.1817)
Pencil on thick cream wove, laid onto heavy white wove card
26.2 × 44.3

Prov: S.D. Kitson, by whom bequeathed, 1939.

The exceptionally meticulous finish of the drawing and the formality of the framing trees is unusual in Turner's work, and might at first sight suggest it was designed for reproduction, but no printed version is known. A larger pencil drawing of Blenheim Palace, set in the wider context of the park, and stylistically identical (private collection, Oxford) is also laid down on the same heavy card as *Conwy Castle*; a similar function, as presentation drawings or possibly as demonstration pieces might be implied. In both subject-matter and style, the drawing looks back to the late eighteenth century and the roots of the picturesque. Its self-conscious stylisation makes it difficult to date. A similar view of Conway of around 1803, after Delamotte, appears in an early sketchbook (Cat.10); but close similarities between the foreground of the related *Blenheim Palace* and *The Vale of Ffestiniog* (Cat.31) may place it within the immediate experience of Turner's Welsh tour of 1816.

Leeds City Art Galleries

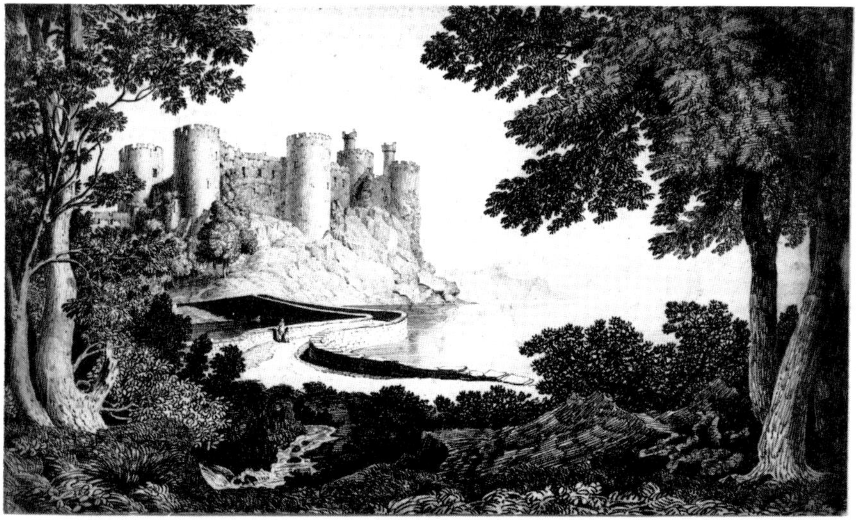

33 A gorge near Castleton, Derbyshire

1818
Pencil, pen and ink on cream wove
28.7 × 22.7
Inscribed *Castleton 1818*

Prov: G.D. Lockett, by whom presented.

The pencil underdrawing was probably made on the spot, while the ink was added later. Turner seems to have appreciated the sparse effect of the initial pencil work, for his later use of the pen can hardly be said to strengthen the composition in the usual manner. Rather, he has simply and accurately reproduced the lines his hand originally traced during the immediacy of his contact with the subject. While this reflects his allegiance to the aesthetic of the sketch with all its emphasis on direct and immediate response, it does not seem anachronistic to suggest he was also capable of recognising beauty in the abstract qualities of lines, which, in such a high-horizoned view, seem simply to wander over the surface of the paper.

The 1818 Derbyshire tour is particularly well represented in terms of the number of surviving drawings. There are several more at the Whitworth, three with the Derbyshire Museum Service and three at the British Museum.

Whitworth Art Gallery, Manchester

34 Portmeadow

(c.1818–20?)
Pen and ink, wash and white bodycolour on blue-grey cartridge
(30.4 × 50.9)

Prov: Percy Manning, by whom bequeathed 1917 (Ms.Top. Oxon. a.21).

The success of this drawing is dependent entirely on Turner's creative vision and technical virtuosity. Emptiness is a distinctive and insistent quality of his work, but nowhere is it suffused with such a powerful sense of the pulse and flow of the elements and of living things. Here it seems to be life itself, in all its power to create, transform, modify and recreate, that powers the elemental flux. This can be sensed in the spontaneous scrawl of underdrawing, and in the organic stylisation of the lines Turner uses to depict the playing children and the vegetation of foreground and horizon. Individual detail is subordinated to overall organisation. Thus the heads of the main figures and the chain of distant trees and buildings are juxtaposed against each other, treated in identical graphic terms.

The Bodleian Library, Oxford

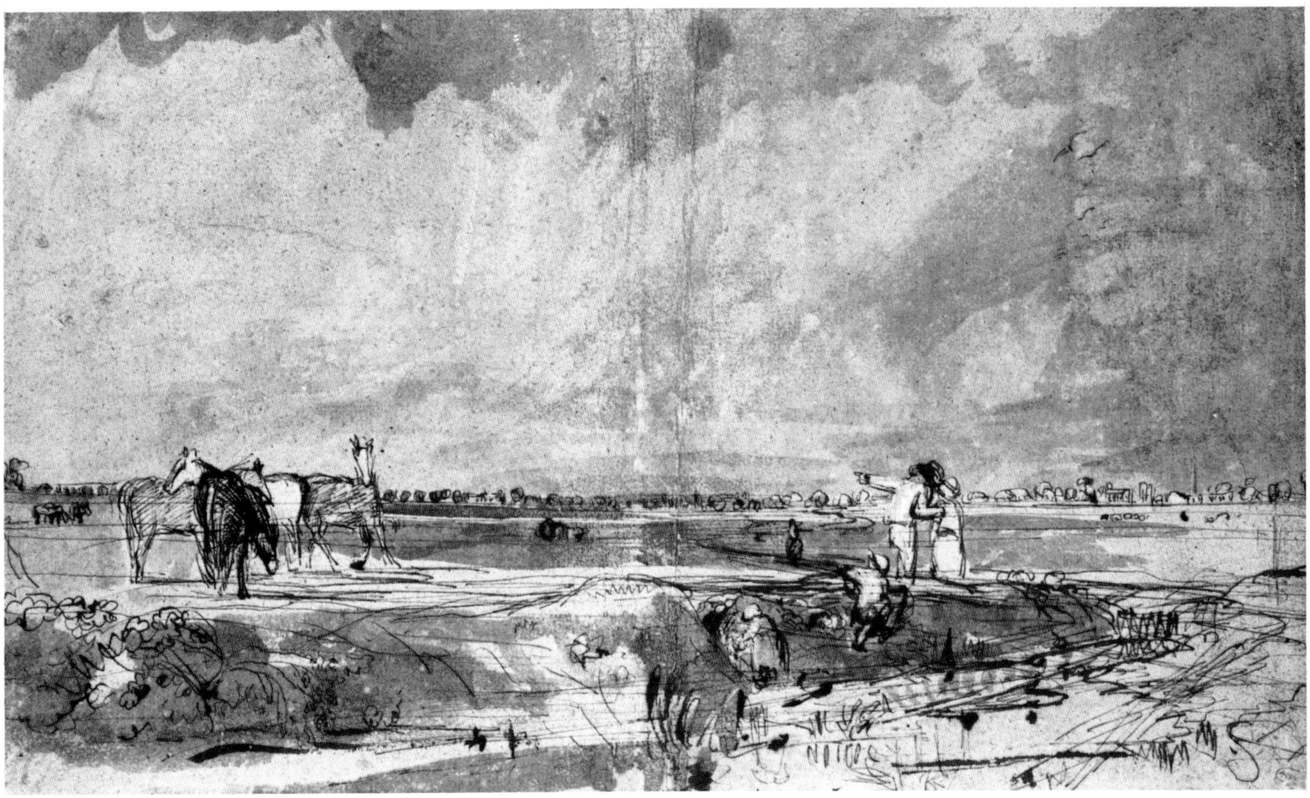

35 A Quarry near Shotover

(c.1818?)
Watercolour and bodycolour on grey wove
24.5 × 43.7
Inscribed on the old mount in an old hand *Quarries at Shotover Hill near Oxford about 1816*

Prov: Fine Art Society 1959, bought Mrs M. Spooner, by whom presented 1979.

Turner's commitment to the pastoral did not make him immune to images of the industrialised landscape. Shotover was one of the few native sources of the pigment ochre. It has not been conclusively proved that the quarry depicted supplied ochre, but this subject would certainly have provoked personal associations for the artist. It may have had a dual attraction, both in its subject and in the visual appeal of the pale rent of the quarry in the dark hillside. He certainly draws attention to the quarry by the impastose bodycolour in a sketch remarkable for the spontaneity of its handling.

The Courtauld Institute Galleries (Spooner Collection)

36 Pit on Shotover Hill

Oil on millboard
27 × 40
(c.1818?)

Prov: The Rev. Canon the Hon. A.F. Northcote; by descent to Sir G. Northcote, by whom presented, 1943.
Exh: UG (3a).

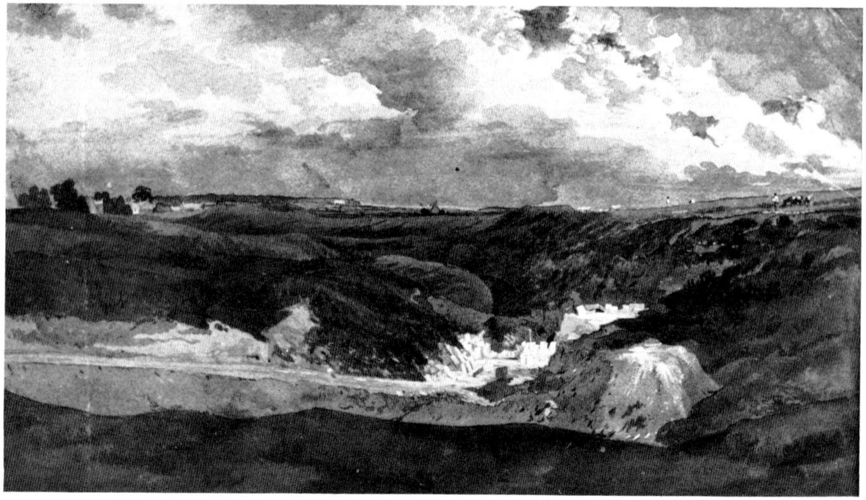

The white-shirted worker and wheelbarrow set against the orangy earth inevitably brings to mind Linnell's *Kensington Gravel Pits* of 1813 (Tate Gallery). However, Turner's approach to this similar subject seems to have been conditioned by some knowledge of Gainsborough's *Landscape with Chalky Banks and Figures* (National Gallery of Ireland; Hayes 13). Whereas Linnell declares his modernity in the frank treatment of toil, here this sense is lost and the worker appears only to be performing a token labour. The most marked similarity to the Gainsborough, is the appearance of the "Dutch" cattle on the skyline; but where there is a single animal Turner here includes a number. The pastoral feel of the Gainsborough is magnified in *Shotover*, at the expense of the social realism.

Reproduced in colour

The Visitors of the Ashmolean Museum, Oxford

37 Study of Sheep

(c.1818–20)
Watercolour and bodycolour on grey wove
27.9 × 46.3

Prov: Squire Gallery, 1958.

A study based on etchings of sheep published by Robert Hills in 1799 and 1808. Most of Turner's animals, cattle and donkeys as well as sheep, were drawn from Hills, copies of whose many portfolios of prints he owned (Studio sale, lot 282). Often content to take only a single animal, here Turner has combined several of Hills' poses in a homogenous group. The sheep are greatly enlarged with respect to their source, and the clean outlines and restrained modelling confer a monumental quality on the flock.

The Ingram Family Collection

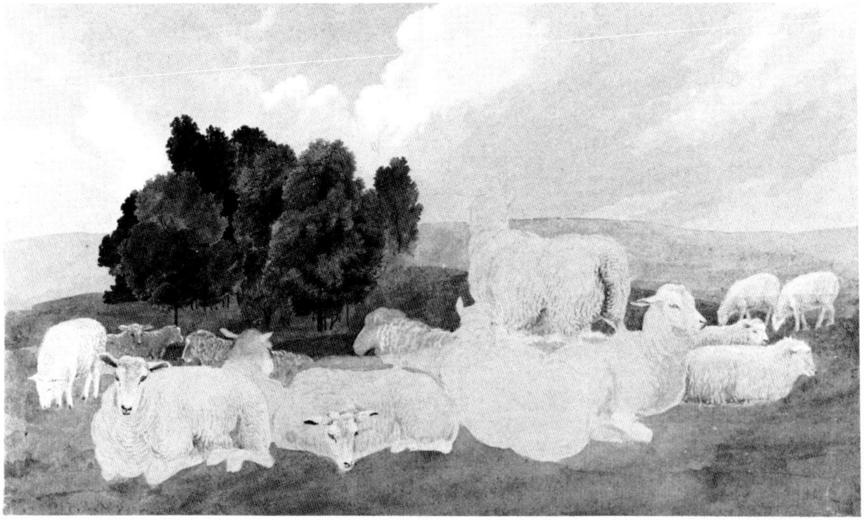

38 St Giles, Oxford

1820
Pencil and wash on cream wove
Signed and inscribed *Near St. John's Coll. 1820 W. Turner*

Prov: Mrs E.T. Leeds, by whom presented, 1957.

Although unfinished, the drawing displays a high degree of stylisation in the flattening effect of the uniform pale wash and the pencil striations. The fretted outline of the foliage, typical of drawings of this period, further enhances the decorative bias of the study.

The Visitors of the Ashmolean Museum, Oxford

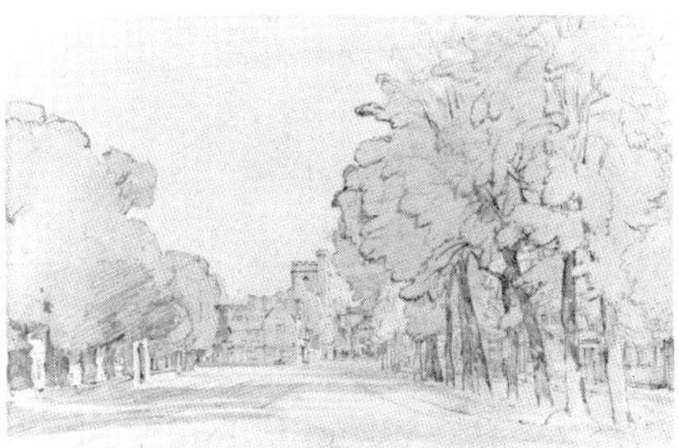

39 Oxford from Headington

(c.1820–23)
Watercolour on cream wove
26 × 40

As a local artist, Turner made many such drawings for Oxford clients. While the skyline is accurate, the foreground presents a conventional image of prosperity (possibly both essential selling points for such clients; compare for example the foreground in *Oxford from Hinksey* (Cat.16) or in *Windsor from near Salt Hill* (Cat.40)). Here, Turner has been so concerned to give the look of "plenty" that he has reduced the figures in scale (even more than in *Windsor*) so that the harvest corn towers high over the heads of the gatherers.

Private Collection

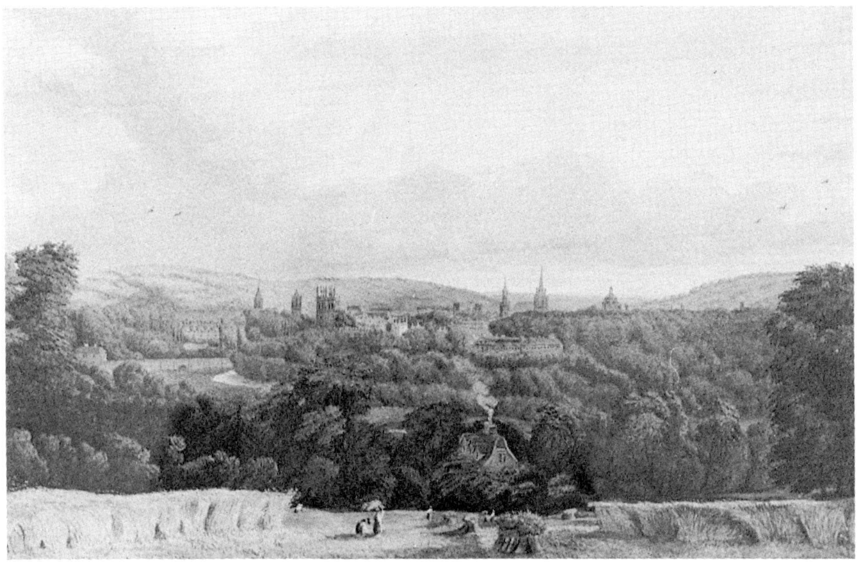

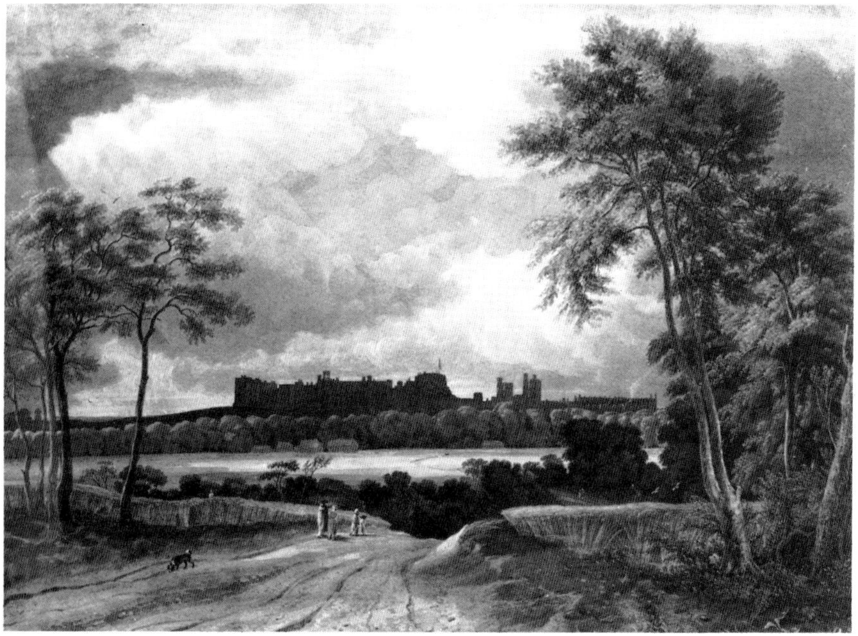

40 Windsor from near Salt Hill

(c.1820–23)
Watercolour and bodycolour on cream wove, cut, scratched and sponged
Signed *W. Turner Oxford* and inscribed verso with title
53.7 × 74.3

Windsor demonstrates a new concern to present detail in a much finer focus. The touches of paint and the cuts or scratches of the extracted highlights individually become much smaller, but in fact their scale in relation to the objects they depict remains the same. This can clearly be seen in the handling of figures. It has to do partly with the demands of the more distant view, but it also results from Turner's deliberate reduction in their scale, a device often found in Girtin and Cozens but much rarer in his own work. The effect aggrandises the seat of the monarch and, when combined with their finer detail, lends to the natural scenery, for example the corn and the trees on the right, a fragile decorative grace. This is particularly evident in the corn below the scratched-out birds. Here observation has given way to a concern for delicate and ornamental design.

Oxford City Council

41 Cilgerran Castle

(c.1820–25?)
Watercolour on white wove
22.8 × 36.8

Prov: F.P. Morrell; by descent.

This drawing is based directly on an early sketch in the Huntington Albums that relates to another album

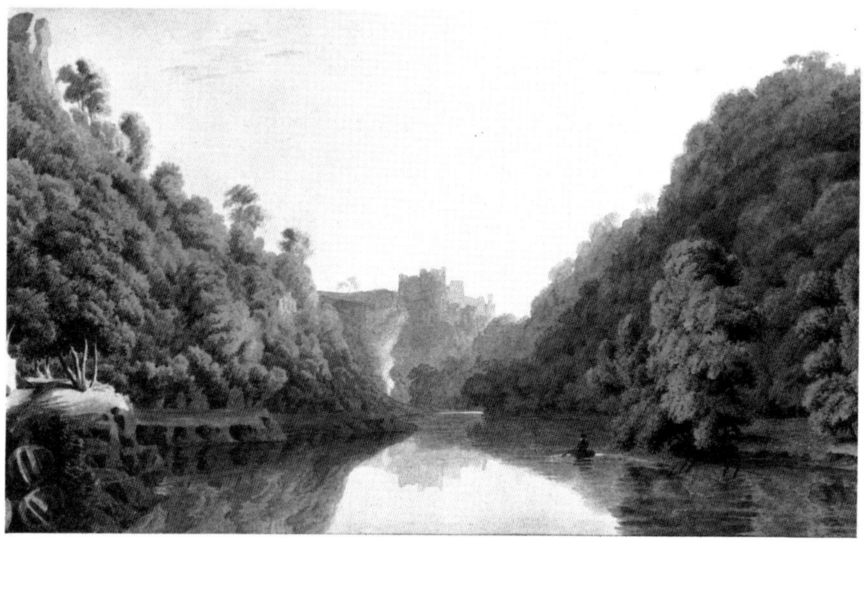

drawing inscribed *Kilgirran Castle*.

The fact that it is directly based on a drawing of some ten years before, and that his earlier drawing is a powerfully silhouetted evening scene demonstrates the ease and skill with which Turner could throw an "effect" over a subject at will.

The striking composition centres the castle at the crossing point of two powerful diagonals. The device of contrasting an object with strong associations of permanent solidity (the castle) with an effect of ephemeral tenuity (the smoke) is one traceable at least as far as the teachings of Turner's master John Varley, who applied the system so rigorously that he attracted censure (see J. Landseer, *Review of Publications of Art*, 1808).

Private Collection

42 Pope's Tower, the Old Kitchen, etc, Stanton-Harcourt, Oxfordshire

1822

Watercolour on white wove

49 × 73

Prov: ?Studio sale, lot 161, £1.6.0 to Bumpstead; Miss Faulkner, 1895; L.R. Phelps, Provost of Oriel College, Oxford; his sale, Provost's Lodge, 2 October 1929, lot 181; Rev. R.H. Lightfoot, by whom bequeathed, 1954.
Exh: SPW 1822 (30); UG (32).
Ref: Herrmann pp.312–318

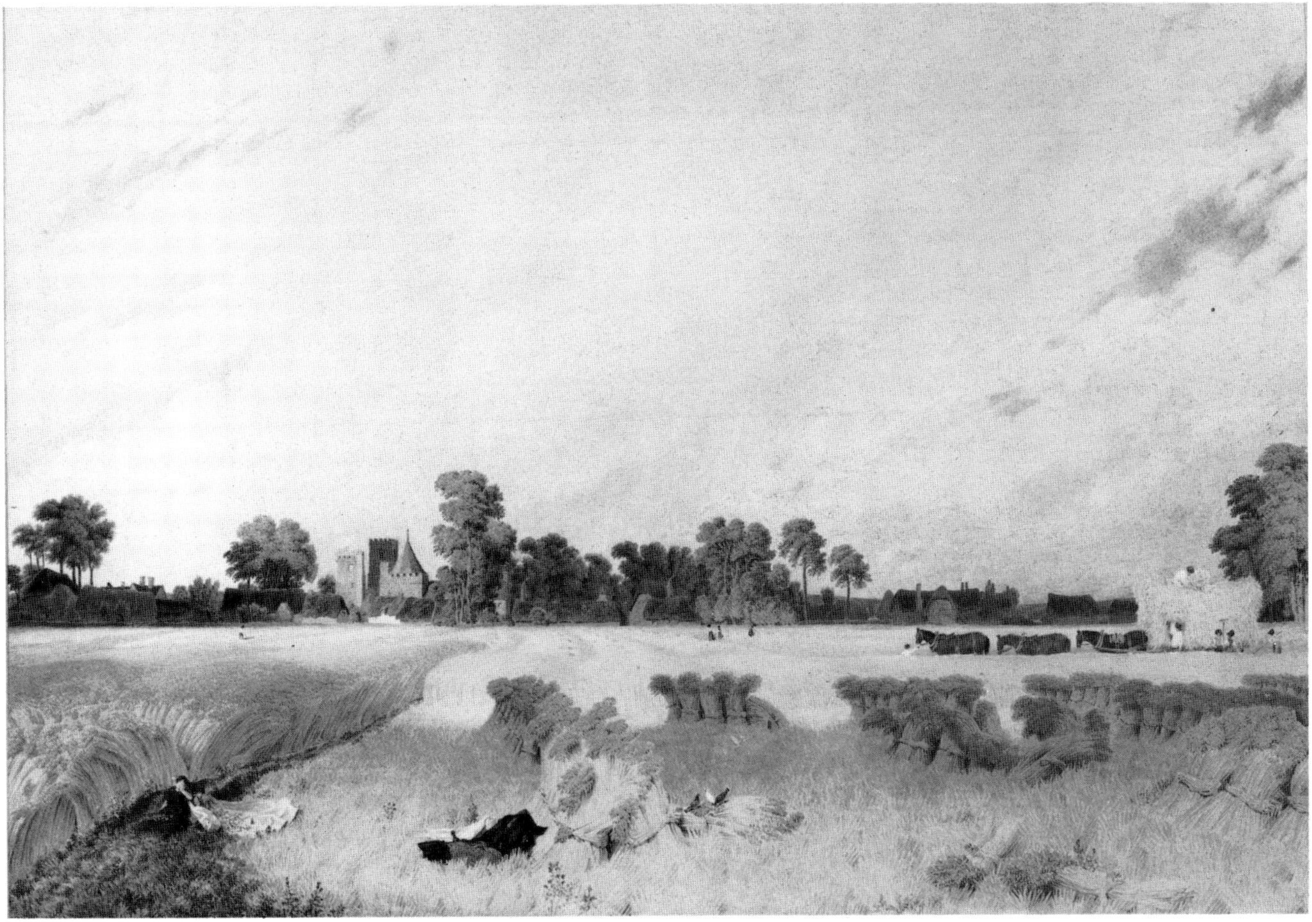

The format of this watercolour of a manor house seen across a harvest field is directly reminiscent of Turner's early treatment of the same subject (Cat.1), but here the scene is completed by the inclusion of the reapers. In contemporary versions of this subject by Cox and DeWint, among others, the figures are often found huddling close to one another and to the stooks, in order to shelter from the wind or rain. Here, it appears that the children are, on the contrary, exhausted by the exertion of picking poppies in the heat. This detail, when added to the sense of volume of the unreaped corn, the groups of plump stooks and the haycart stacked almost to overflowing becomes in sum not only a scene of a bounteous harvest, but an image proclaiming the sufficiency of contented work and an emblem of "Plenty". It is perhaps no co-incidence, in view of this sense of heat and surfeit, that the buildings in the distance are Pope's Tower and the great kitchen of Stanton Harcourt Manor. The largest and most complete medieval domestic kitchen in England, it has been described as one big oven; Pope compared it to the forge of Vulcan: "The horror of it" he says "has made such an impression upon the country people, that they believe the witches keep their sabbath here, and that once a year the Devil treats them infernal venison, viz. a toasted tiger stuffed with tenpenny nails" (J. Sherwood and N. Pevsner *Oxfordshire, The Buildings of England*, 1974, p.783).

For illustration see p.49

The Provost and Fellows of
Worcester College, Oxford

3. 1824–c.1840

On 5 July 1824, at the age of 34, Turner married Elizabeth Ilott, seven years his senior. She came from a family of small landowners from Broadwell, virtually the next village to his native Black Bourton. The couple had no children and there is no evidence that the event altered significantly the pattern of his life and work, although various members of Elizabeth's large family crop up as pupils and buyers.

At about this date one of Turner's cousins acquired a farm in the New Forest, and he appears to have spent a great deal of time there, studying at first hand the source of much of Gilpin's *Remarks on Forest Scenery*. Contemporary accounts of the forest make much of its poor management, and the large amount of dead wood; this was one of the eminently picturesque features which appealed to Turner. The variety of trees standing in sparse clumps in the heathy land dotted with pools of water are directly reminiscent of Jacob van Ruysdael and Hobbema. It is probably from this base that Turner was able to begin to explore the South Downs, which first appear in exhibited works in 1834.

In the following year Turner continued his exploration of expansive, lowland landscape in a tour of the Thames valley, which took him as far as Rochester and the mouth of the Medway. The sketches made on this trip (e.g. Cat.54; two others are in the Sadler Bequest, Oxford Town Hall) are remarkable for their sheer size, and also their shape. Their long, low format (which is parallelled occasionally in Robson and DeWint), its lateral extension suggested by dispensing with typical framing trees, surely owes something to the panorama. Panoramas, 360-degree painted views, set up in specially constructed buildings, were an immensely popular form of entertainment at this date. But whereas the viewing-platform of the panorama provided a point of vantage from which to identify the many landmarks, Turner's views, though topographical in origin, compress their subject-matter to a minimal strip of mid-distance, and seem to aspire to a featureless landscape.

This tendency in his work was remarked upon as early as 1824, when the reviewer of the Literary Gazette wrote: "This is an unusual scene, and treated in an unusual manner. Long level lines, a flat surface, and a low tone of colouring are forced by the skill of the artist to become not only sweet, but picturesque. It is quite a triumph of art" 1 May 1824, p.283). The work was entitled *Scene near Oxford – November 1st, 1823*, and its subject was the flooding resulting from the violent storms which swept the country on 30–31 October. ("Waters out" Turner noted for this work in his copy of the SPW catalogue.) The work is now lost, but is noteworthy in its combination of topicality, novel treatment, and depiction of the uncontrollable forces of Nature.

In the later 1820s, there was considerable controversy in the ranks of the Watercolour Society concerning the use of bodycolour (for a full account, see Bayard, pp.21–23). It is interesting to find Turner noting in 1827, a year in which Havell was particularly censured for violating the purity of the watercolour medium, that his own *A Woodman's Cottage* was "partly body colour"; in general, though, he was extremely sparing in its use. The solid, opaque whites of Harding or William Henry Hunt are never found in his finished work; mixed with colour, bodycolour is reserved only for the final details enlivening the foregrounds of the large exhibition pictures. Where Turner is unusual is in his preference for bodycolour, usually greatly diluted with watercolour, as a sketching medium. By this means he was able to achieve quickly the strength of colour built up so painstakingly in the overlaid watercolour touches of the large works. Equally discrete in his use of gum, and almost totally eschewing the rubbing, sponging and scraping of many of his contemporaries, Turner remained as much of a traditionalist in technique as he was in regard to his subjects.

Respect for tradition prevailed, too, in Turner's one known venture in architecture. In 1831 H.J. Passand, an old friend of the Turner family (who was to marry Turner's cousin), became rector of Shipton-on-Cherwell. The opportunity was taken to rebuild the village church, then in a delapidated state, and Turner became its architect. A later rector recorded the widespread acknowledgement of the fact that "all the details of the old church were faithfully copied, including the tracery of the windows" (noted in 1885, Shipton Parish records, on deposit in Oxfordshire County Record Office). Some fragments of the original fourteenth-century sculpture were incorporated, notably in the South chancel window.

43 Self-portrait

(1824?)
Oil on paper on canvas
55 × 38

Prov: Rev. T. Archer Turner, 1895; by descent to Mr C.E. Turner, by whom presented, 1932.
Exh: UG, second issue (1).
Ref: Herrmann, p.246.

Although portraiture provided the staple income for many nineteenth-century landscape painters, from Constable down, Turner almost never engaged in the practice; apart from a watercolour portrait of his uncle (family collection) this self-portrait represents his only known effort in the genre. The tradition of marking a marriage by a portrait was very well-established, and is presumed to have provided the incentive on this occasion. In view of Turner's lack of experience as a portrait painter, one is reluctant to draw conclusions from the pronounced vertical orientation and stiffness of the whole performance.

See frontispiece for reproduction

The Visitors of the Ashmolean Museum, Oxford

44 Exeter College Garden

(c.1825–30?)
Watercolour and some gum with scraping out on white wove
27 × 37.5

This unassuming watercolour is representative of many small views of the Oxford colleges produced by Turner throughout his career. The discarded roller and basket are typical of the informal detail found in all of Michael Angelo Rooker's engravings of similar subjects for the *Oxford Almanack* (1770s and 1780s); the warm evening light casting long shadows over the lawn is Turner's own unmistakeable contribution.

The Rector and Fellows of Exeter College, Oxford

45 Exeter College Eight

(c.1826)
Watercolour with some gum and rubbing out on white wove laid down on card
31.5 × 50.4

Inscribed verso *Henry Moresby's Eight Oxford/Son of Fairfax Moresby, Stow House Litchfield/and my uncle, M.F. Moresby, 1881*

Prov: ?Henry Moresby: ?presented to the Boat Club by his nephew M.F. Moresby, 1881.
Ref: *The Field*, 23 March 1912, repr.

This recently rediscovered watercolour, although in a badly damaged state, has considerable historical significance. It appears to be the prototype for a great number of watercolours of rowing crews produced by Turner and probably duplicated by his pupils. The model was subsequently adapted in prints by other artists where the standard form is most often found hand-tinted with the colours of a particular college.

Henry Moresby, the stroke of this crew, was one of the leading figures in

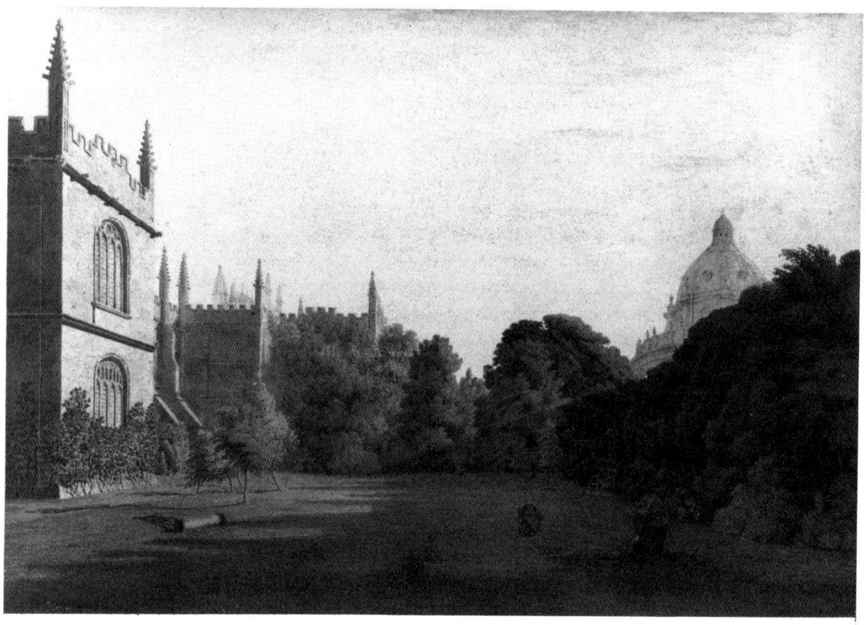

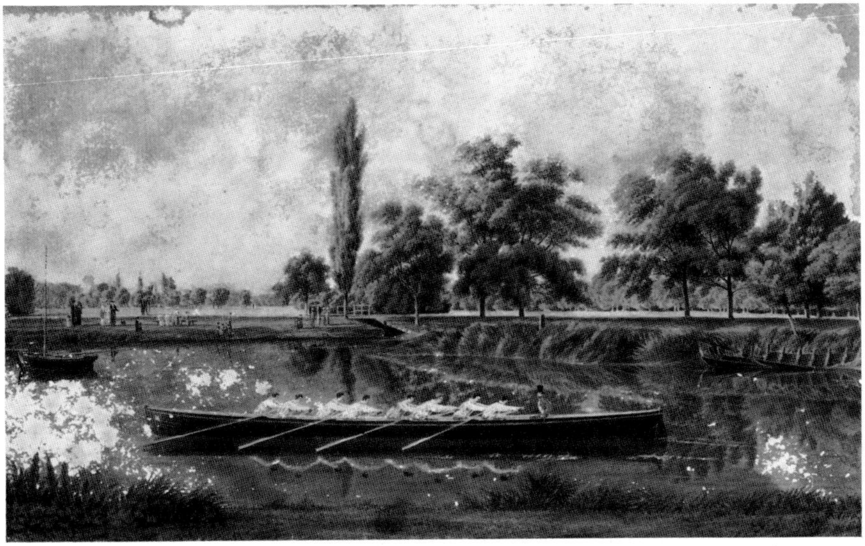

George Fennel Robson was commissioned by Mrs Haldimand "to form a representative album of drawings by the best watercolour painters of the day" (Roget, vol.1, p.464), and at the Annual Exhibition of the Watercolour Society in 1827 the contributions of all the leading members of this album were shown together as a separate group. Turner's response to the occasion was to produce a watercolour which would hold its own beside the best efforts of the contemporary masters, and fully represent his own special talent. The strong contrasts of light and dark in the sky and on the land, and particularly the unusual step of casting the central plane in deep shadow are designed to be eye-catching and create real drama in spite of the restricted scale.

Mr Michael Danny

the early days of Oxford rowing. In 1824, he was responsible for having Exeter College's famous and highly successful "White Boat" built in Plymouth. The boat depicted here is a replacement, first raced in 1826, the year in which Moresby and others drew up the first formal rules for University racing.

Exeter College Boat Club

Cat.45

Cat.46

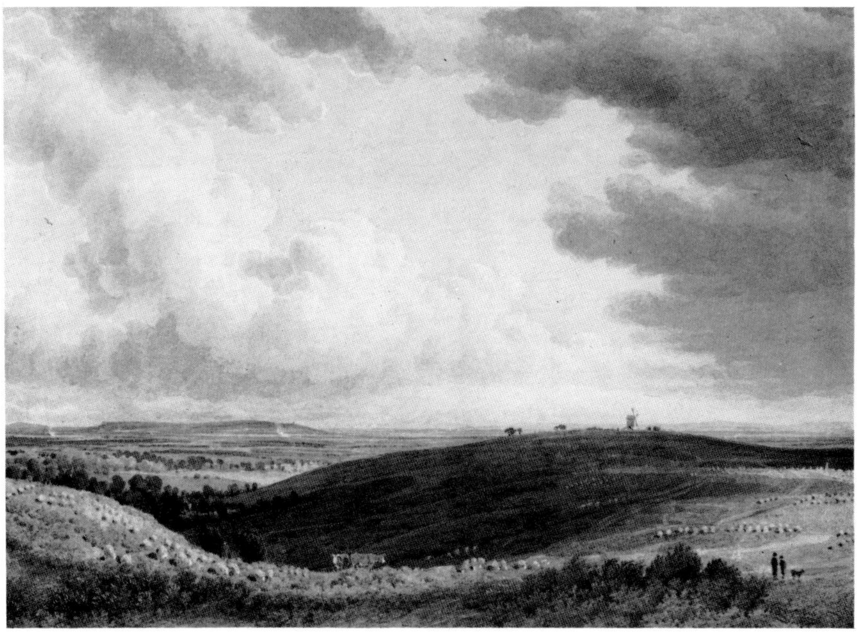

46 Shotover Hill

1827
Watercolour on white wove
18 × 25

Prov: Mrs G. Haldimand; her sale, Christie's, 21 June 1861, lot 80, bought Agnew's; Christie's, 18 March 1980, lot 281.
Exh: SPW 1827 (337); J.&W. Vokins Gallery 1883; J.&W. Vokins Gallery, *Loan Collection of Watercolour Drawings representative of the English School*, 1891 (111).

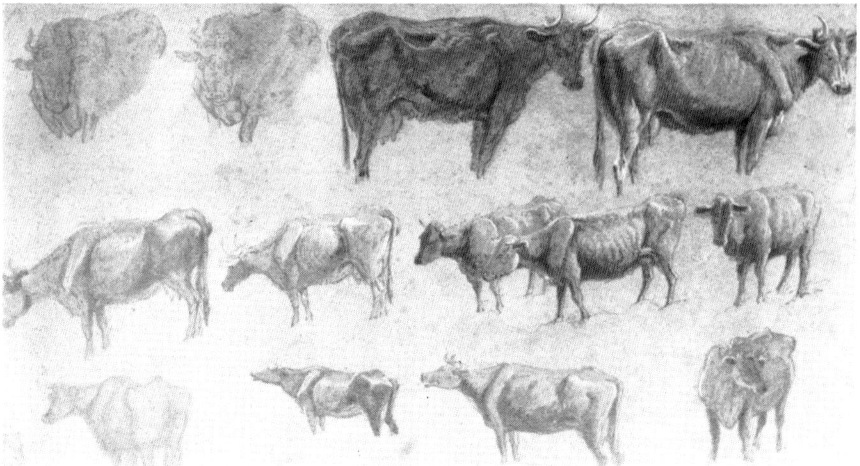

47 Studies of cattle

(c.1830?)
Watercolour and bodycolour
22.2 × 40.6

A sheet of studies based on Hills' etchings of cattle published in 1801 and 1804. Here Turner is experimenting with colour, and with slight variations in lighting and posture.

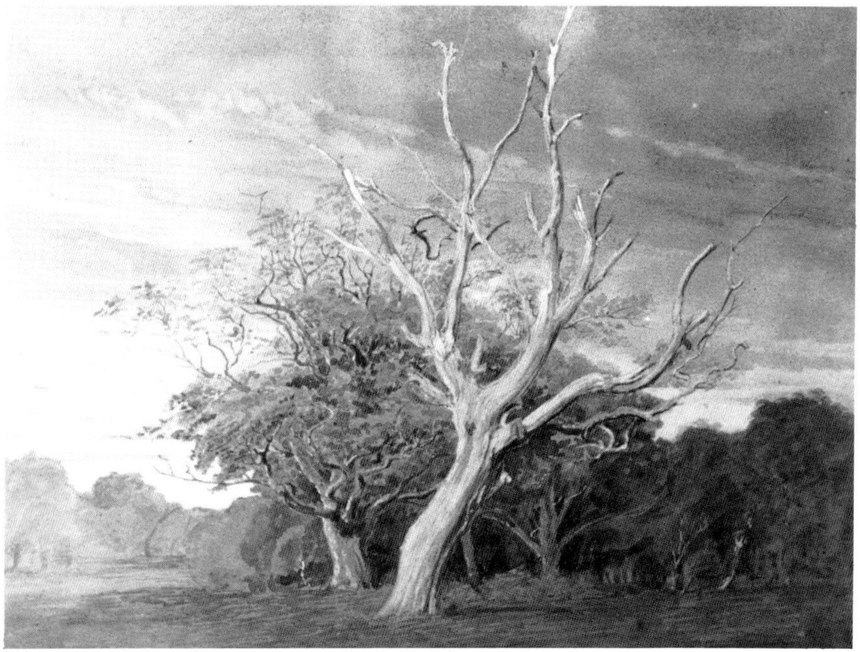

Stylistically, a dating in the early 1830s seems feasible. The cow in the top right appears in a New Forest view of about this date (Ashmolean Museum). However, the pair of cattle in the middle row is used in a view of Alnwick Moor dated 1850 (University College, Oxford).

Private Collection

48 Study of an oak tree in the New Forest

(c.1830?)
Watercolour and bodycolour
36.4 × 27.8

An early example of Turner's looser sketching style. The foreground tree was incorporated into a large New Forest watercolour dated 1831 (Agnew's 1972; private collection).

Private Collection

49 Boating on the Isis

(c.1830–35)
Watercolour on white wove
20.5 × 32.6

Prov: Michael Bryan 1982.

The view of the spires of Oxford from the banks of the River Thames was painted by Turner on numerous occasions, but he was never so successful in marrying it with the evocation of the elements. Before college rowing became firmly established in the 1820s, sailing was a very popular undergraduate pastime. This stretch of the river was well known for its squally and treacherous conditions: "Boats were to be seen swamped . . . nearly every day in the October term", James Pycroft recalled (*Oxford Memories. A retrospect after fifty years*, 2 vols, 1886, vol.2, p.74). In its simple contrasting of a limited number of pictorial elements and communication of personal knowledge and experience, this image is wonderfully expressive of the greatest aspects of Turner's art.

See catalogue cover for colour illustration.

Private Collection

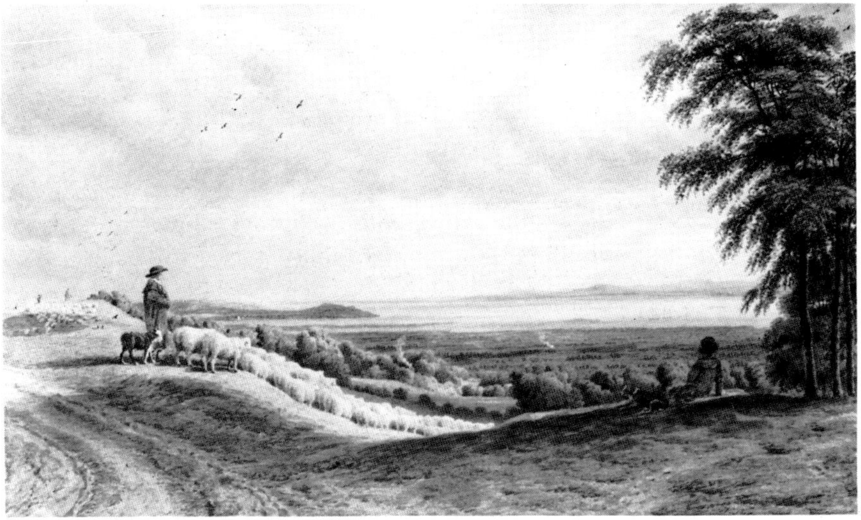

50 View from King's Weston Down near Bristol looking towards King's Road

1832
Watercolour on white wove
24 × 39
Signed *W. Turner* and inscribed with title on reverse

Prov: M. Routh (1755–1854), President of Magdalen College, Oxford; by descent to E.M. Lee; Agnew's 1984.
Exh: SPW 1832 (104), 5 guineas.

Of all the widespread unrest which accompanied the passing of the Reform Bill through Parliament, the Bristol Riots of October 1831 saw the largest crowds and were by far the most violent, sending shock waves and murmurs of revolution throughout the country. In view of Turner's response to the Otmoor riots of 1830 (see Introduction), it is possible that the decision to exhibit a Bristol view at this moment, unique in his work after the group of 1810–15, was influenced by current events. Turner's apparently timeless depiction of a single shepherd and his dog gains a special piquancy when the surrounding social upheavals, which appeared at the time more threatening than they eventually proved, are considered. The city itself is kept out of sight to the right, but all our attention is focussed in that direction, and not only by the gazes of the foreground figures. Both the wind and the light come from there, and it may not be fanciful to dwell on the discomfort of the shepherd who wraps his coat around him in the face of the north-easterly blast.

Thos. Agnew & Sons Limited

51 Clovelly, North Devon

(c.1833)
Watercolour and scraping out
28.8 × 45
Signed and inscribed verso, *Clovelly, North Devon. W. Turner*

The coast of North Devon and Cornwall, with its cliffs and rocky coves, attracted many artists from the end of the eighteenth century. Turner's first view in the area was a painting of Lynmouth, exhibited in 1823, and many others followed during the 1820s and 1830s, although towards the end of the period it was the wilder and more dramatic parts of the Cornish coast which occupied his attention. This work is a reduced variant of one probably exhibited in 1833 (Mellon Center, Yale); lack of any information other than the title makes a positive identification impossible. Another similar view of

Clovelly, but showing more of the village seen from the edge of the sea is in the Huntington Library. This type of coastal scenery forms an extreme contrast with the flat, extensive, South coast landscape which Turner was also investigating at this time. Dispensing altogether with a foreground, Turner launches his viewer into the midst of the waves, wanting to recreate the immediacy of the experience of the elements which is so crucial a part of life in the tiny fishing village.

Mr Robert Mills

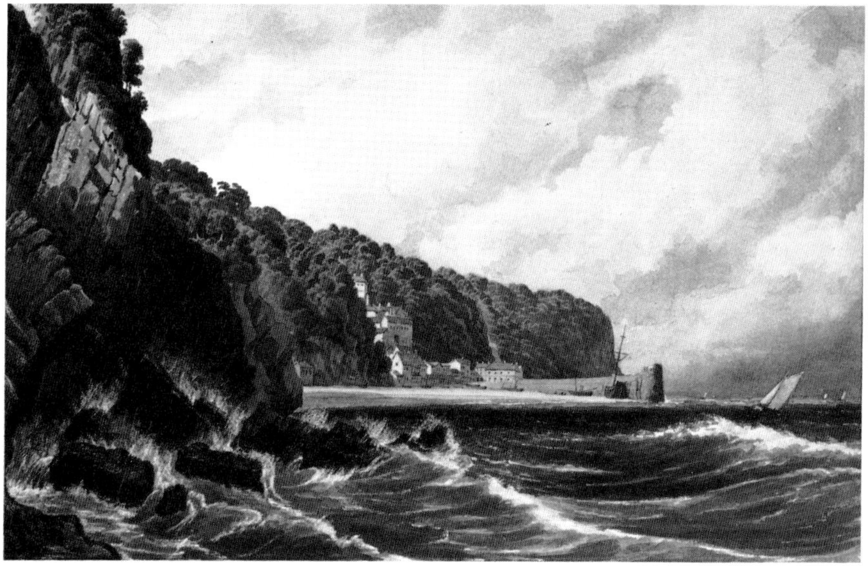

52 Landscape with approaching storm

(c.1830–35)
Pen and sepia; brush and indian ink heightened with white bodycolour on grey paper
25 × 42.8
Signed *W. Turner*

Prov: D. Percy; purchased 1942.
Ref: Herrmann, p.244, repr.

A considerable number of similar studies exist, largely relating to finished work of the 1830s and 1840s. All are hastily executed, noting down an idea for a dramatic sunburst or shower, they are often in a named locality. They represent an intermediate stage between the precise topographical sketching and the elaboration of the exhibition watercolours.

This drawing is complicated by the fact that the sheet was used twice. Firstly, for a pen drawing of Harlech Castle (closely related to a watercolour c.1830 in the Laing Art Gallery, Newcastle), then for the storm effect. The figures are echoed, in reverse, in the large watercolour, Cat.53.

The Visitors of the Ashmolean Museum, Oxford

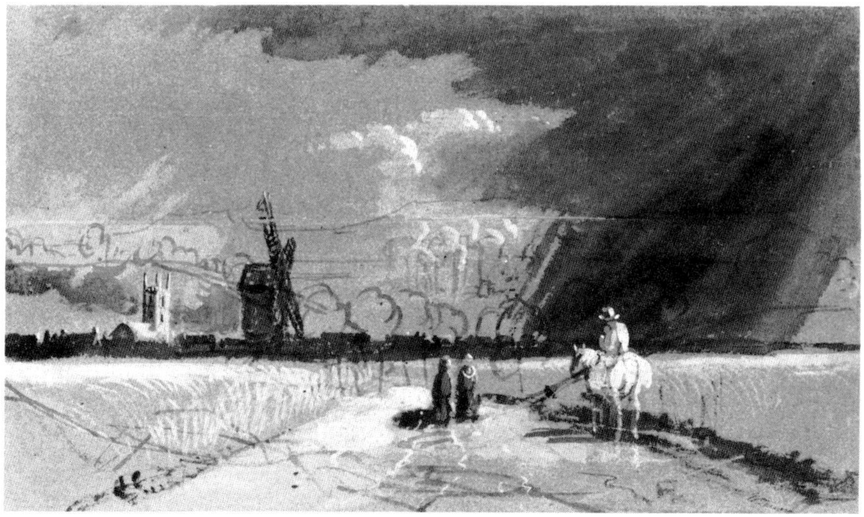

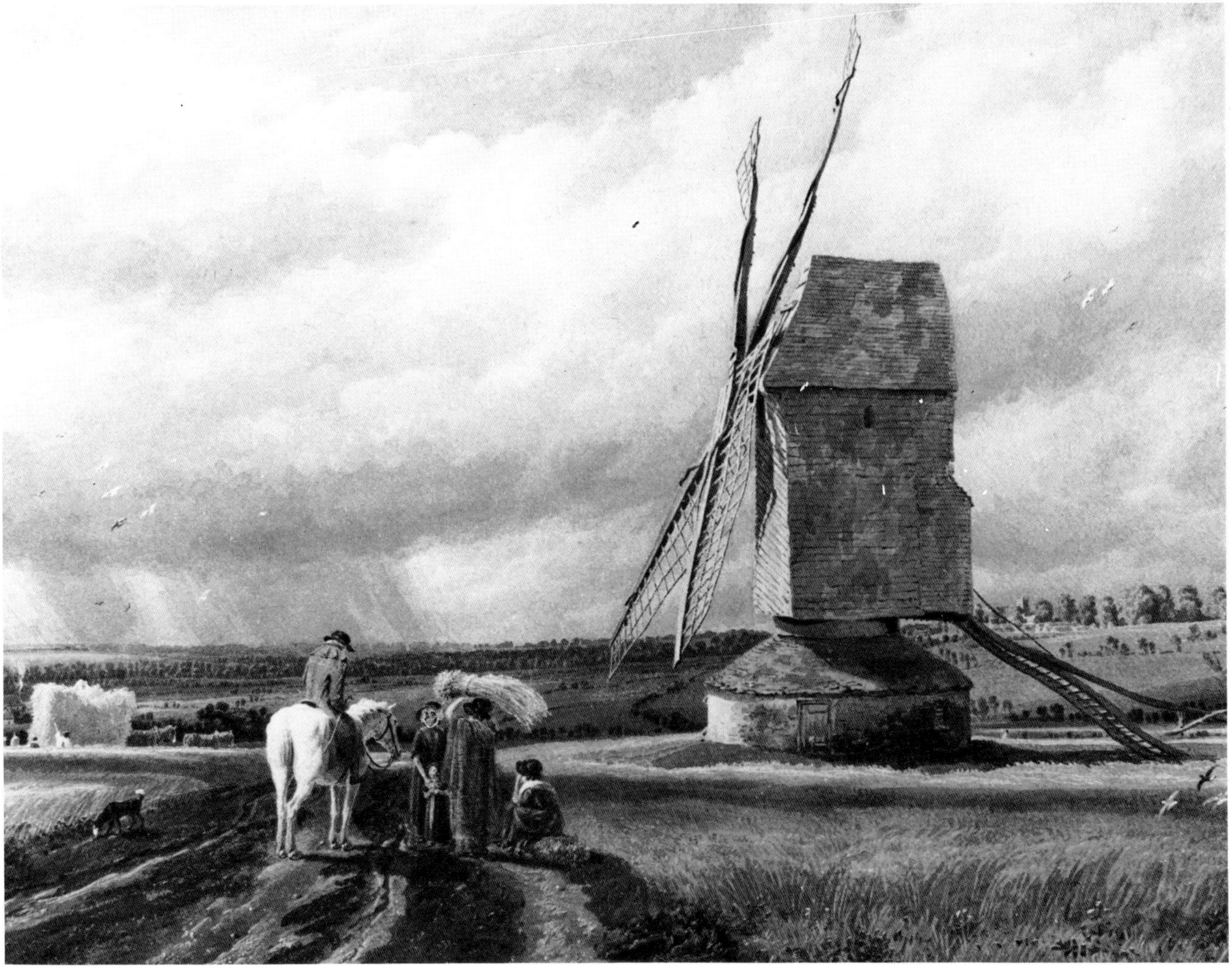

53 Landscape with windmill in a cornfield

(c.1830–35)
Watercolour on cartridge
53.5 × 67.7

Prov: Presented by C.E. Lees, 1888.

This is more likely to be a pastiche of favourite motifs than a specific location. A near identical watercolour reproduces all the scenic elements, but substitutes a church spire for the tower, far right (Sotheby's, 30 March 1983, lot 149).

This is one of Turner's most precisely articulated images of the ideal peace and plenty of the countryside. The men pile the wagon high with corn, while the proprietor converses benignly with a woman and her children, who are returning laden from gleaning. The cloudy sky evokes the power of the wind, which will drive the windmill to grind the corn into flour for bread.

Oldham Art Gallery

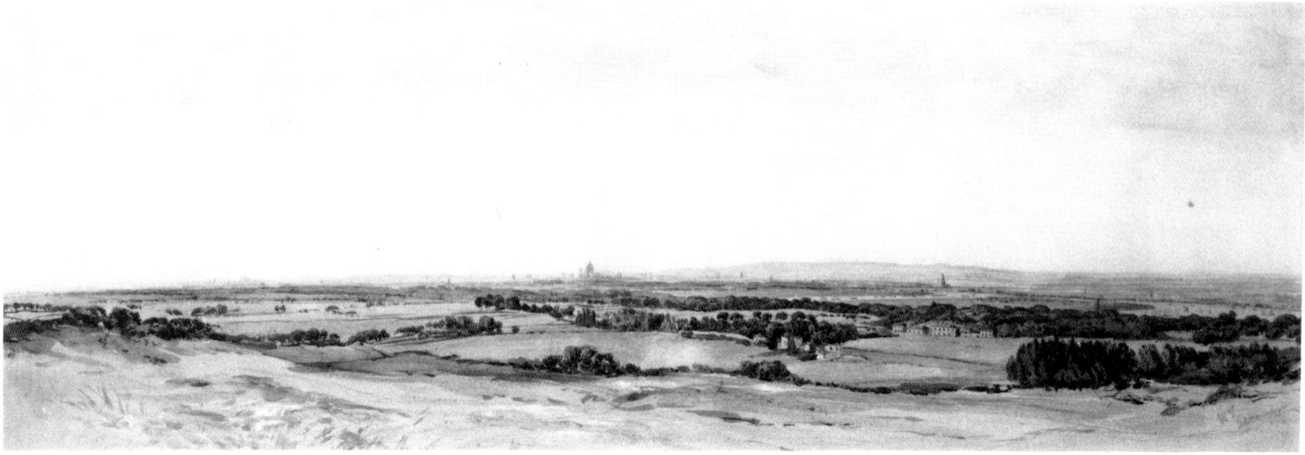

54 London from Shooter's Hill

1835
Pencil, watercolour and bodycolour on buff paper
25 × 74
Signed *W.T.* and dated *July 22 1835*

Prov: James Dole, 1892; Lord Broadbridge; Sotheby's, 30 November 1978, lot 129; Spink's.

Despite its size, this distant view of London was certainly drawn on the spot, even if coloured later. It demonstrates Turner's growing interest in open, expansive scenery, which is partly reflected in the increasing scale of some of the exhibited works. Although he is not known to have based a finished picture on this sketch, Turner did exhibit a view of Portsmouth Harbour in oil measuring well over six feet wide at the British Institution in 1841.

Morgan Grenfell & Company Limited

55 A pollarded willow

1835
Watercolour with some gumming and bodycolour on buff paper
37.3 × 27.1
Inscribed verso *Godstow Oct^r.13 1835*

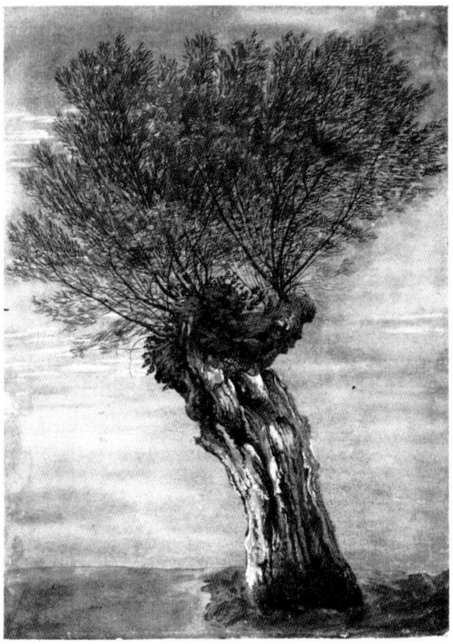

Prov: Christie's, 14 May 1968, lot 10; Fine Art Society; Helen Barlow, March 1969, by whom bequeathed, 1975.
Exh: National Gallery of Scotland, Edinburgh *English Watercolours and Other Drawings. The Helen Barlow Bequest*, 1979, Cat.48, repr.

Willows recur in Turner's paintings of the River Cherwell with water lilies, but it is curious he should have made this careful study at Godstow, several miles from Shipton. Depth of colour is his principal concern; the tinted paper was washed with blue before the tree was begun, its darker greens and browns further strengthened by the admixture of very dilute gum. In its precision of colour and form, it is strongly reminiscent of oil studies made by John Linnell when under Varley's tuition, thirty years earlier.

The National Gallery of Scotland, Helen Barlow Bequest

56 Eel traps on the Cherwell

(c.1835)
Watercolour with some gumming and bodycolour on buff paper
14.2 × 21.8

One of the most brilliant of Turner's studies of the Cherwell, amply demonstrating how the extensive use of bodycolour is not inconsistent with the greatest delicacy. Both stylistically and technically, the study can be closely associated with *A Pollarded Willow*, dated 1835 (Cat.55).

Reproduced in colour

Private Collection

57 Two girls resting by a cornstook

(c.1835?)
Watercolour and bodycolour on buff paper
15.8 × 22.4
Signed and inscribed *Study from Nature. W.T.*

Prov: Rev. Archer Turner; Rev. L.R. Phelps; ?his sale, Provost's Lodge, Oriel College, Oxford, 2 October 1929, lot 167 (part); Helen Barlow, by whom bequeathed, 1975.
Exh: National Gallery of Scotland, Edinburgh, *English Watercolours and Other Drawings. The Helen Barlow Bequest*, 1979, Cat.47, repr. in colour.

The free handling of this sketch, which incorporates numerous pentimenti, is comparable with dated sketches of the mid 1830s. Similar figures recur in a watercolour of Dunstanborough (Sotheby's, 11 November 1982, lot 89).

The National Gallery of Scotland, Helen Barlow Bequest

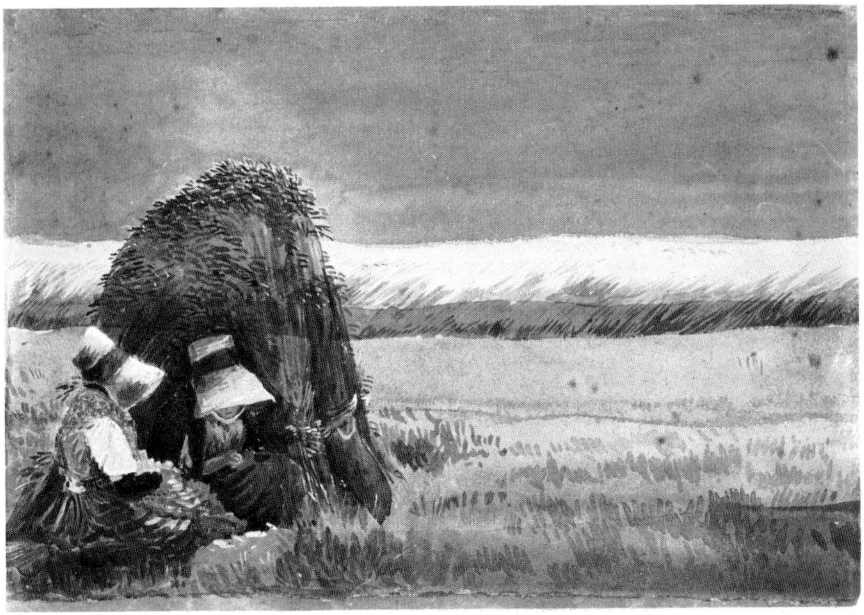

58 Heath Scene near Beaulieu in the New Forest

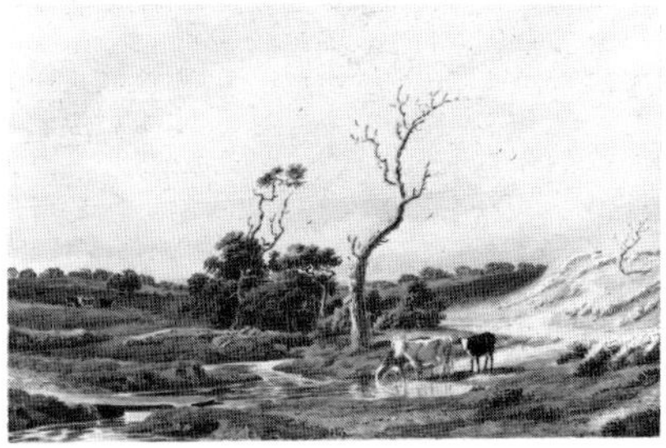

1838
Watercolour on white wove
28 × 41.9 (a vertical strip 3.5cm wide added to the right)
Signed *W. Turner/Oxf*^{d}. Signed, inscribed with title and address, *16 St. John's Street. Oxford* on old label

Prov: W. Wells, 1838; Albany Gallery, 1975.
Exh: SPW 1838 (226).

At a period when he was experimenting with richer pigments and unusual lighting effects, Turner could still look back to the purity and economy of means of the eighteenth century. The limited colour range, the use of the white of the hard paper for highlights and the glazed blue washes create an archaic aura which, from what we know of the rest of Turner's work at this date, must be self-conscious, suggested by this archetypically picturesque imagery.

Mr David Fothergill

59 Portsmouth Harbour from Portsdown Hill

(c.1840)
Watercolour and bodycolour
59 × 99
Signed *W. Turner Oxford*

Prov: C.E. Lees; by descent to Mrs E. Prodgers; Lawrence of Crewkerne, 17 November 1977, lot 9; Richard Green; Christie's, 16 March 1982, lot 131.
Exh: Manchester, *Royal Jubilee Exhibition*, 1887 (1660); Preston, *Guild Art Exhibition*, 1902; Manchester, Whitworth Institute, *Loan Exhibition of Watercolour Drawings*, 1912 (102).
Ref: *Country Life*, vol.CLXIII, 12 January 1978, p.78, repr.

Turner exhibited versions of this view in 1834 (SPW (19); Christie's, 30 June 1981, lot 127), 1840 (RA (525), in oils, private collection, England) and 1841 (British Institution (244)). Other versions, including this very large watercolour, are known, making it one of his most popular subjects.

During the Napoleonic Wars, Portsmouth was Britain's largest and most important dockyard and naval base. It remained for painters and public alike a focus of British sea-power; paintings and prints of the harbour crammed with ships struggling under a fierce wind are common throughout the first half of the nineteenth century. For Alison, "National associations [increase] the emotions of sublimity and beauty, as they very obviously increase the number of images, presented to the mind" (Alison, p.23). Since the wars ended in 1815, Portsmouth saw a marked decline, and by 1840 was already virtually eclipsed by Southampton. Turner's interest in the subject at precisely this period seems to stem from a delight at seeing this military centre reverting to a state of nature; the Royal Academy work was specifically entitled *View of Portsmouth Harbour in the time of peace*. The associations of the place are important, but their strength acts as a foil, bolstering by very contrast the serene expansiveness of Turner's view.

The pair of standing sheep in the bottom right corner are copied from Hills (see also Cat.37), and are found in a great number of Turner's works. The group is even duplicated here by the next pair to the left.

Reproduced on page 8

Private Collection

4. 1838–1862

The art of Turner's middle years was ruled by a desire to discover a harmonious balance among the forces at work in nature; the final phase of his career has another distinct character, typified by dramatic effects and private emotion, and is ushered in by the tour of Scotland undertaken in 1838. Turner was nearly fifty when he made this lengthy journey. Although inscribed and dated drawings show him in the Lake District in 1840 (Cat.65) and Northumberland in 1844 and 1847, he does not appear to have repeated the Highland tour. Nonetheless, Scottish subjects came to form a major part of the output of the remainder of his career.

Turner's route took him through many of the well-known sites, but he went further than most visitors (judging from the many contemporary guide-books) and seems to have preferred the wilder, more remote parts. By 5 July 1838, he was already beyond Inverness; a drawing inscribed Loch Croisk (for Chroisg; Cat.60) documents him in that tract between Inverness and Loch Maree which was the setting of a number of late works. He continued even further north, to Loch Inver, before turning southward via Loch Torridon to Skye, whose hills and coast he explored thoroughly. Back on the mainland, the main road south would have led him along the side of Loch Garry, and on through Glencoe, which he reached by 4 August. And so on, past the more familiar shores of Loch Lomond, painted in two near-identical works in 1839 (SPW (247)); Phillips, 23 March 1981, lot 110) and 1848 (SPW (99)); Leger Galleries, 1983).

Scotland did not provide Turner with material which would dramaticlly extend the range of his subjects beyond that derived from English sites. The *View from Querang* (Cat.62) is comparable to the South Downs views of about the same date; *Loch Coruisk* (Cat.61 & Cat.81) is no more dark and stormy than views of *Tintagel* (Worcester College, Oxford, repr. OWCS Annual IX, pl.iv) or one from *Pordenak Castle, Cornwall* (SPW 1837; Fine Art Society) and the weeping birches of *Loch Garry* (Cat.82) evoke a similar atmosphere to the weeping willows of the Cherwell. This is not to say that Turner was unable to respond to the specific character of the Highlands; in one important respect Scotland embodied the theme treated so persistently in the English lowland subjects: it sustained the myth of a landscape uncontaminated by any human influence, and it did so more convincingly than ever in England.

It is still possible, however, that the initial trip and the subsequent proliferation of Scottish subjects owe more than a little to the strength of the market. Turner almost admits as much in writing to the Secretary of the Watercolour Society about his submission to the Manchester Art-Treasures Exhibition, when he says his "drawings of Mountain Scenery . . . of late seem to be preferred by my friends" (3 January 1857; SPW Ms).

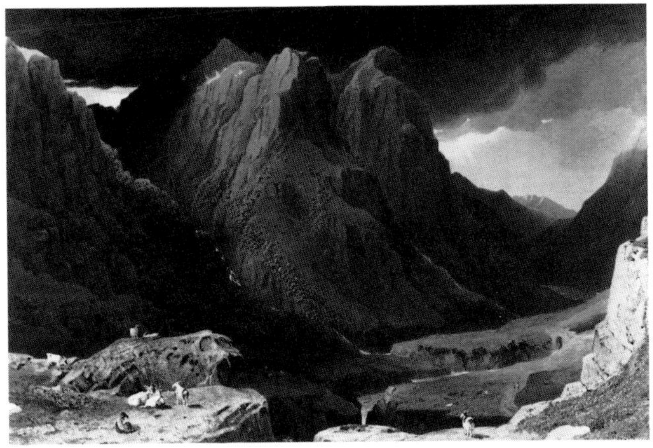

Fig. 5 George Fennel Robson (1788–1833). *The Pass of Glencoe* 1820s? Watercolour. City of Manchester Art Gallery

The scenery of Scotland became popular with tourists and artists slightly later than the Lake District and North Wales. During the first half of the nineteenth century, however, the volume of visitors increased enormously. Although Gilpin had written about the Highlands, he was not entirely enthusiastic, seeming to sense his efforts to systematise overcome by the scale of the subject. The terms of Scotland's appeal were broader, and addressed more directly to the imagination than were the the theories of the Picturesque. The Scotland which so captivated the popular spirit was that defined, or even created, by the works of Walter Scott. *The Lady of the Lake* (1810), set around Loch Katrine in the Trossachs, and *The Lord of the Isles* (1815), set on the West Coast and Skye, provide grandiose scenery with appropriately romantic and heroic narrative. The blend was so persuasive, that most of the scenes Scott depicted remained forever in his imaginative grasp, which provided a framework of associations through which the English tourist learnt to interpret the scenery.

While many of Turner's fellow watercolourists follow Scott's lead to the letter, Robson and Cristall being foremost among them, Turner himself attempts at least to let the land speak more for itself. It is impossible to escape from the overtones of Scott, precisely because they are so in tune with popular expectations of the associational landscape; Turner's continuing emphasis on the original emptiness of the Highlands is a strong-willed imaginative gesture in its own right, and a valid corrective to the over-familiarity bred by Landseer and his many followers on the walls of the London exhibitions.

The price-books of the Watercolour Society show that Turner commanded no higher prices at the end of his career than at the beginning. During the 1840s the prices even dropped slightly. Where the reputations of the stars of the Society grew, and with it their prices, Turner settled into the role of an "also-ran", consistently "creditable", but receiving only rare mention from critics. Lacking the technical virtuosity of a Cox or a Fielding, he was easily overlooked, even by Ruskin. His reference to "the quiet and simple earnestness, and tender feeling, of the mountain drawings of William Turner" was added only to the 5th edition of *Modern Painters I* (1851; 4th ed., 1848). The situation had been no different twenty years earlier; the writer of the *Library of the Fine Arts* in 1831 accompanied his praise of Turner with considerable special pleading on behalf of his "sober style": "his works are not only unobtrusive, but even uninviting, appearing at first sight rather sombre than gay, and to be known must be sought" (vol.1, no.6, June 1831, p.513). Even in mid career, Turner's absence from London appeared to have stalled his true development and critical recognition; he was apparently forgotten by the Society and omitted from the *Gallery of the Society of Painters in Watercolours*, published from 1831 to 1833, a short-lived attempt to publicise members' work through engravings. In later life Turner consistently refused invitations, and, while he remained on good terms with the Society, showed no desire for participation or exchange of ideas. His reply to an invitation from the Secretary of the Society in 1857 is categorical: "for some years past I have gone very little from home, and dinner parties have been entirely declined" (SPW Ms). In these circumstances, is it entirely surprising that in the catalogue of the Leeds International Exhibition of 1868, his dates are given as "about 1770–1840"?

From 1831, Turner lived modestly in St John Street, which was then inhabited by tradesmen, college servants and teachers, with a good many student lodgers. The census records that he kept a maid; after his wife's death in 1851, her elder sister Mary lived with him, and she is the principal beneficiary of his will. Shortly afterward, in 1853, Turner's uncle also died, and the manor of Shipton-on-Cherwell was let, to be sold eventually by his son in 1862. The date of that sale was the date of William Turner's death: 7 August 1862. His long association with the place, most especially as the setting of the late series depicting the water-lilies on the Cherwell, so much a private sanctuary, makes the coincidence all the more poignant.

60 Loch Chroisg, Inverness-shire

1838
Watercolour and bodycolour on buff paper
10.8 × 21
Inscribed *Loch Croisk. 5 July 1838*

Prov: Maas Gallery; Albany Gallery; Sanders of Oxford.

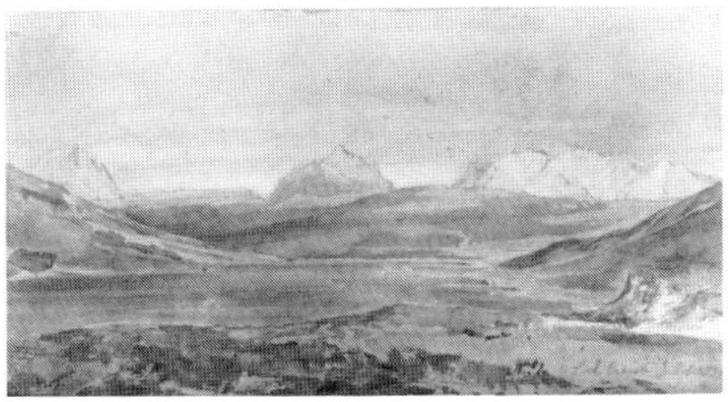

One of a number of dated sketches made by Turner during his 1838 tour of the Highlands. It is most likely that he followed common practice and drew only the pencil outline on the spot. The colouring, added later, serves as more than a mere aide-memoire, though; its delicate and discrete application creates space and atmosphere.

Private Collection

61 Loch Coruisk, Isle of Skye, at Sunset

(c.1838)
Watercolour and bodycolour
33.1 × 55
Signed, inscribed with title

Prov: H.S. Theobald; Maas Gallery.

Loch Coruisk, on the western coast of the Isle of Skye, provided many painters and poets with a most perfect example of the sublime; vast, rugged, and impenetrably dark. Scott's journal contains a full account of his visit, concluding: "though I have seen many scenes of more extensive desolation, I never witnessed any in which it pressed more deeply upon the eye and the heart than at Loch Corriskin; at the same time that its grandeur elevated and redeemed it from the wild and dreary character of utter barrenness" (*The Lord of the Isles*, 1830 ed., note XXXII).

This study, presumably elaborated in the studio, does not over-emphasise the emotional potential of the scene; rather, the painter seems to delight in the variety and subtlety of colour binding the stormy sky and bare rock.

Reproduced in colour

Private Collection

62 View from Querang, Isle of Sky, the Mountains of Garlock, Applecross and Kintail and Islands of Rona and Raasay in the Distance

1839
Watercolour with traces of gum and bodycolour and some scratching out
55.2 × 45.7
Signed *W. Turner. / Oxford.*

Prov: Studio sale, lot 109, £4.10.0d. to Newman.
Exh: SPW 1839 (8), £20.

With *The Vale of Glencoe*, also exhibited in 1839 (Cat.63), this watercolour dates from immediately after Turner's return from the Highlands. Together, the two works show the variety in subject, and corresponding handling,

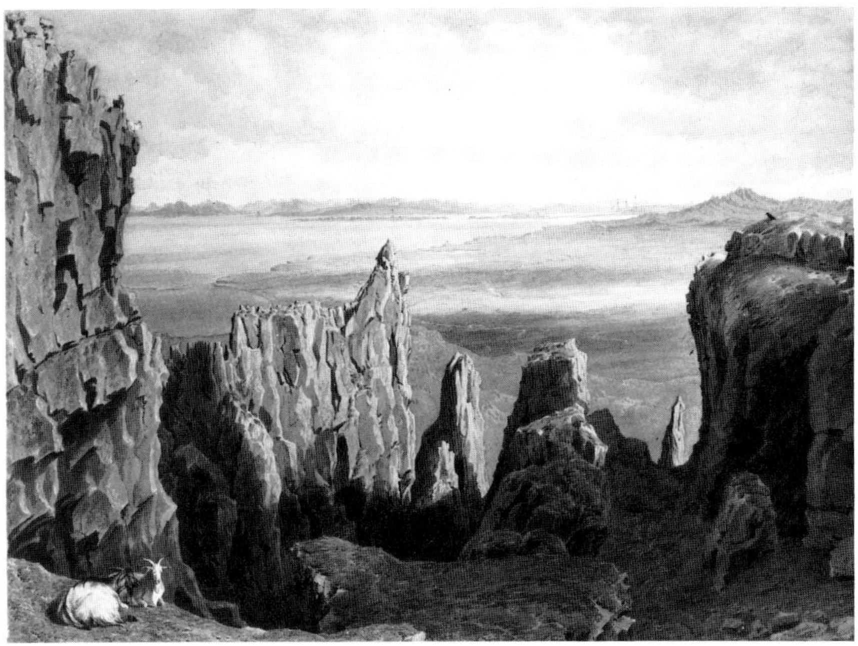

possible in large and small pictures in a single year. In the *View from Querang*, relatively broadly painted in flat washes of colour, Turner found the expansive subject so favoured on the South Downs, with the added eccentricity of the bare stone columns. By contrast, *Glencoe*, finely touched, presents a more conventional image of tranquil rusticity.

Private Collection

63 The Vale of Glencoe

1839
Watercolour
40.5 × 64.9
Signed and inscribed on old backing: *The Vale of Glencoe Near Loch Leven Argyllshire. W. Turner Oxford*

Prov: G. Thompson, 1839; by descent to Sir John Thompson; Buckell & Ballard, 7 June 1982, lot 493, bought M. Bryan.
Exh: SPW 1839 (95), *Sold*; UG(57).

Another work from the first group of Scottish subjects to be exhibited.

Of all the places in the Highlands with historic associations, Glencoe, scene of the infamous massacre of the MacDonald clan in 1692, was one of the most potent. Most writers of the nineteenth-century guidebooks, recalling the event, emphasise the hostility of the place. The watercolours of G.F. Robson dating from the 1810s and 1820s (see fig.5) well illustrate an

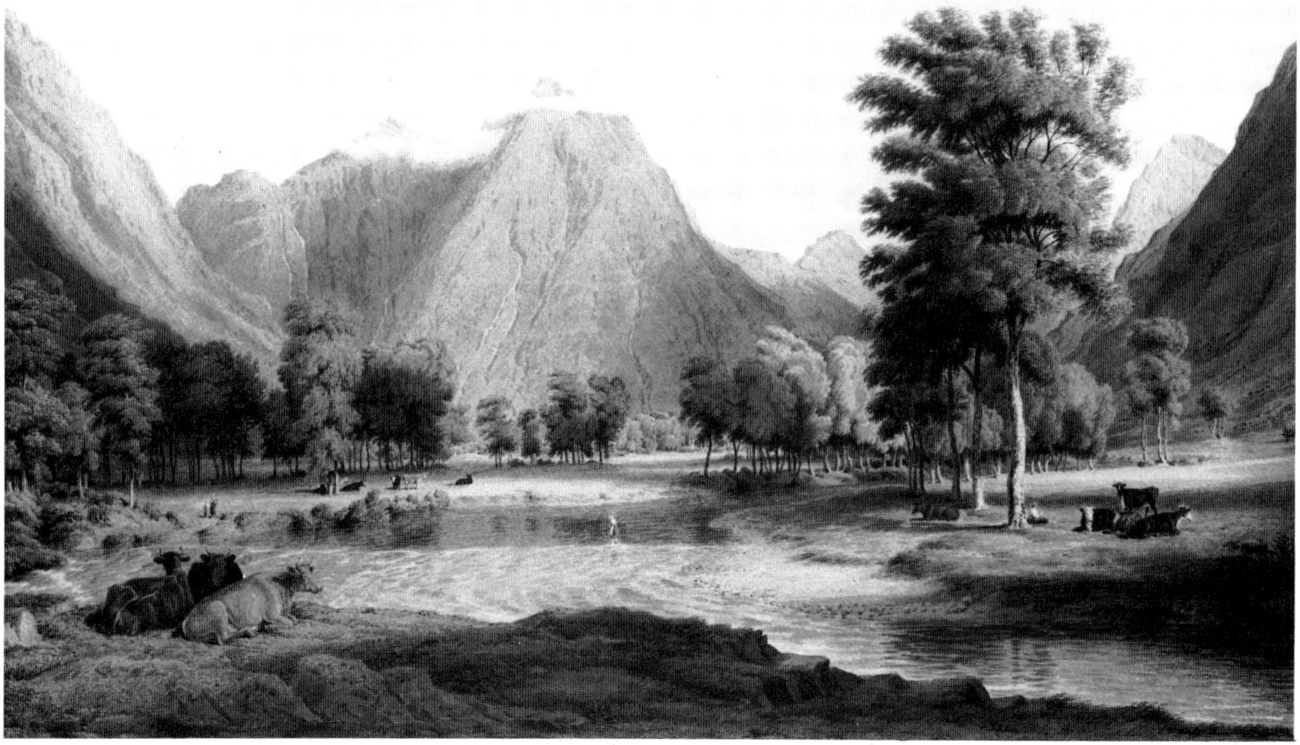

attitude still current much later in the century in descriptions such as J.P. Lawson's in his *Scotland Delineated* (1847–54): "Lofty, sharp and serrated precipices rise in frightful and savage nakedness on the north . . .". While in Glencoe, Turner did in fact produce a drawing identical to Robson's view (dated *4 August 1838*; Castle Gallery, Kenilworth), but he was also capable of a more personal reaction, as is demonstrated by this image of an idyllic haven, discovered further along the valley, which seems to subvert typical expectations of the scene.

Mr Michael Bryan

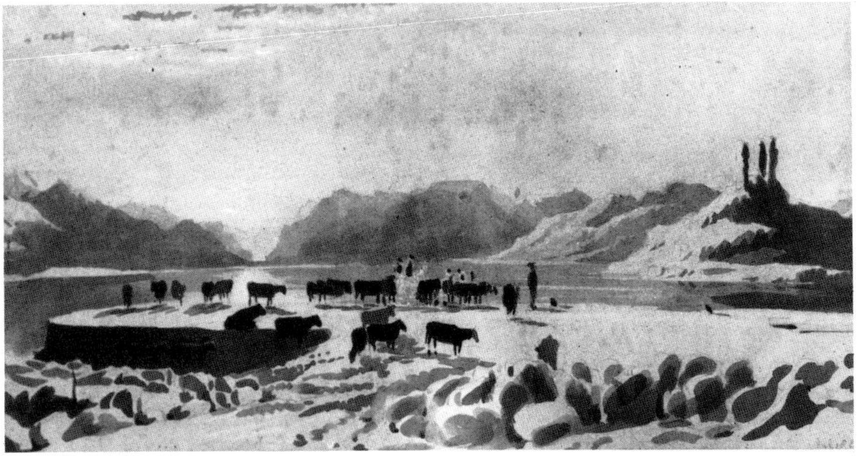

64 Drovers waiting for a ferry

(1838–?)
Sepia heightened with white bodycolour on buff paper
21.1 × 43.3
Inscribed *July 1838*

Prov: Sir Michael Sadler; presented to the City of Oxford, 1931.

A sketch which from the obvious speed of its execution may well have been begun in front of the subject. It corresponds in all details to a large watercolour which has been entitled *Highlanders and their cattle near Caisteal Maol on Loch Alsh* (Sotheby's, 19 March 1981, lot 115, repr.). The grouping of the figures and cattle and the addition of the wash was presumably the result of a later reworking, in preparation for the larger composition. The sight of drovers waiting for the ferry from Skye to the mainland, on their way to the great trysts which took place in late August and September, was one Turner would certainly have witnessed.

Oxford City Council

65 Keswick from the side of Skiddaw

1840
Pencil with touches of white bodycolour on grey paper
25.6 × 37.5
Signed *W.T.*, inscribed with title, and ?in another hand: *Castlerig* (top row) *Ashness, Shepherd Crag, Grange Crag, Glaramard, Yew Crag, Scawfell Pike*, (bottom row) *Barrow House, Wrynose, Bowfell, Castlecrag, Catbell*

Ref: Grasmere and Wordsworth Museum, *The Lake District Discovered, 1810–1850*, 1983, p.51.

The drawing belongs to a group bearing dates in July 1840, which constitutes the only documentary evidence of a return to the Lake District since the initial visit of 1814. Turner may have gone in search of the mountain scenery which so captivated him in Scotland, but the many Lake District views which appear in subsequent years are almost all routine productions, and lack the imaginative spark of the best Scottish subjects. Obviously made with future paintings in mind, the drawing is a stunning feat of visual concentration. No detail seems to have escaped the artist's eye, yet the view is recorded with both clarity and breadth.

The Clonterbrook Trustees

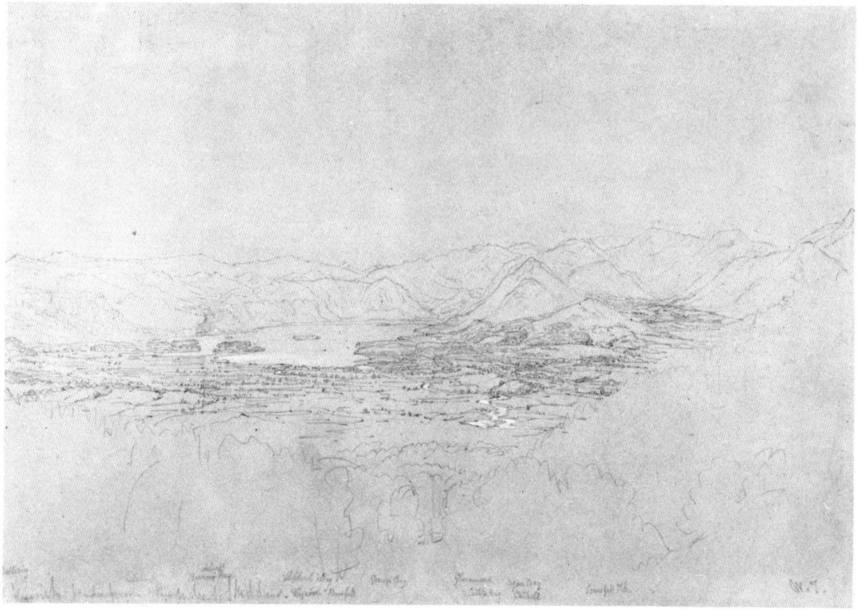

Cat.65: Keswick from the side of Skiddaw

66 Oxford from Headington Hill

(c.1840–45?)
Watercolour with some gum
34.4 × 53

Prov: A.E. Anderson, by whom presented, 1928.
Exh: Reading Museum and Art Gallery, *Paintings of the Thames Valley*, 1968, Cat.25; Queensland Art Gallery, *etc*, *Town, country, shore and sea*, 1982–83, Cat.67, repr.

One of the most popular views of Oxford, and painted by Turner on several occasions. The foreground is very carefully finished; particular attention has been paid to the sculptural massing of the trees and the fall of the light, which adds its own glow to the golden autumnal foliage. The pervading stillness is perhaps overemphasised to the point of freezing the scene. Turner's special exertion is possibly in response to an important local commission; a view of Magdalen College, Oxford, still in an Oxfordshire collection, is remarkably close in style and atmosphere.

The Syndics of the Fitzwilliam Museum, Cambridge

67 Ewelme

1843 or 1845
Watercolour and white bodycolour on grey paper
22.3 × 36.5
Inscribed *Ewelme / July 22 184– (–3 or –5?)*

Prov: F.P. Morrell; by descent.

This delicate sketch of an Oxfordshire village shows Turner at his most

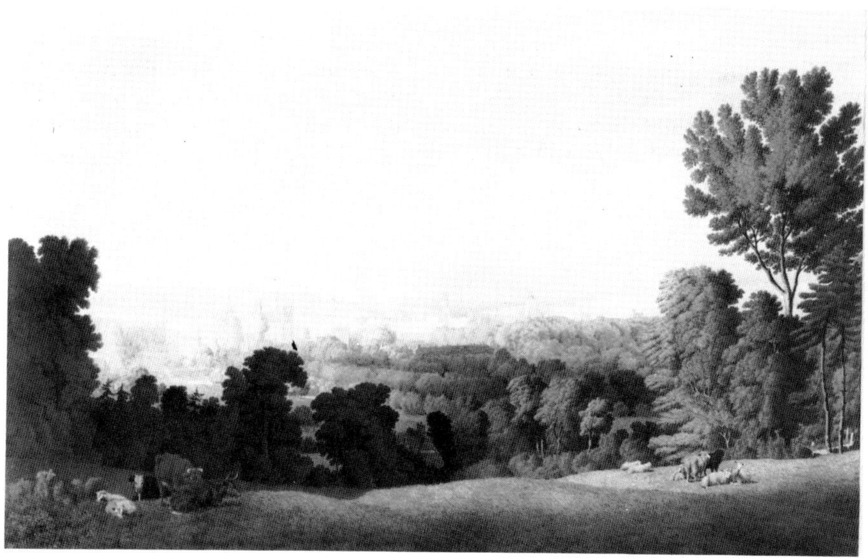

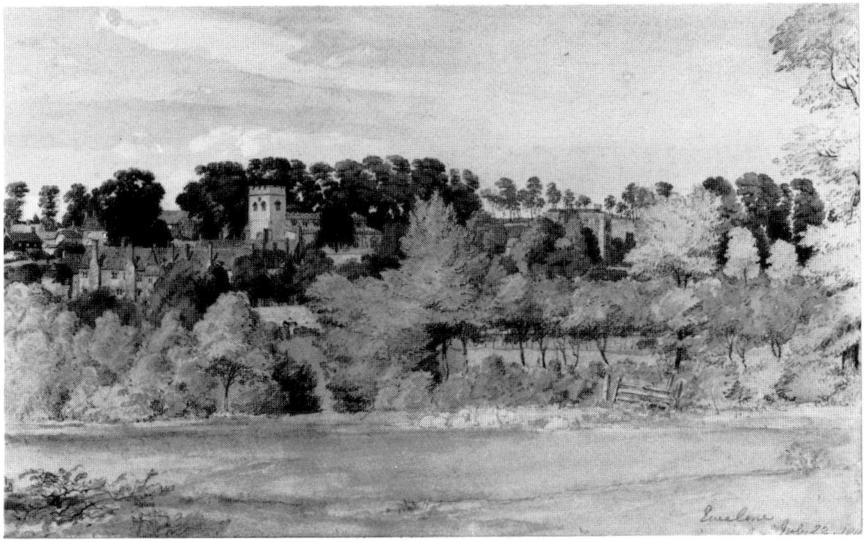

informal. The freely overlapping washes create an effect which is almost entirely decorative, and seemingly independent of the underdrawing.

Private Collection

68 View from Bow Hill, on the South Downs, near Chichester – Langston and Portsmouth Harbours, and the Isle of Wight in the distance

1846
Watercolour with touches of bodycolour
44.4 × 84.7 (including a strip 1.5cm deep added to lower edge)
Signed *W. Turner / Oxford*. Signed and numbered *N°6* on verso

Prov: ?C. Stone; N.D. Newall; his sale, Christie's, 13 December 1979, lot 79.
Exh: RA 1846 (1150); British Council, *British drawings and watercolours in the People's Republic of China*, 1982, Cat.67; Royal Scottish Academy, Edinburgh, *British watercolours and drawings from Rowlandson to Riley*, 1982, Cat.58.

Despite its title, it is difficult to see this work as topographical in any established sense of the term. The foreground does not serve the presentation of the distant view but usurps its place as ostensible subject of the picture; the formal pairing of the cloudy blue sky and pale golden cornfield is so striking as to admit the distance only as an intrusion. Essentially, the image is two-dimensional, and any dynamic accents are underplayed in the desire to present a moment of perfect equilibrium. The edges of the cut corn, such an important element in many other paintings of the harvest field, are softly merged with the overall tonality and the figures, confined to a single narrow plane, stretched like taught elastic across the surface. The sky, sculpted in layer upon layer of the most transparent wash, may have lost a little of its original sharpness; its present lack of real definition only reinforces the self-effacing character of the whole work.

Reproduced in colour

Private Collection

69 Stonehenge, stormy day

1846
Watercolour and touches of bodycolour with some scraping out on cartridge
45.7 × 67.8
Signed and inscribed on the reverse
N°5. Stonehenge – Stormy Day.
W. Turner. 16 St. John Street Oxford

Prov: H.C. Green; Sotheby's, 18 October 1961, lot 180, bought Colnaghi; purchased, 1961.
Exh: SPW 1846 (184), £15, *sold*; British Council, *British drawings and watercolours in the People's Republic of China*, 1982; Royal Scottish Academy, Edinburgh, *British Watercolours and Drawings from Rowlandson to Riley*, 1982, Cat.59.
Ref: Herrmann, p.245, repr. p.244.

Stonehenge was a popular subject with artists in the nineteenth century. It excited a range of reactions, but was still generally acknowledged as an outstanding example of the Sublime. J.M.W. Turner included it in his *Scenery of England and Wales* (*Stonehenge*, published 1829), and Constable exhibited a large watercolour of it in 1836 (see L. Hawes, *Constable's Stonehenge*, 1975, for a full discussion of this and other representations of the subject).

William Turner exhibited a distant view of Stonehenge under the title

Salisbury Plain – Showery Day in 1838 (Chatsworth; a variant dated 1839 is in the Ashmolean Museum). The power of the monument seen close-to demanded a much more dramatic "effect", in accordance with the principle enunciated by Constable in his *English Landscape* (1833). In his commentary to the print *Old Sarum*, he wrote "The subject of this plate . . . is grand in itself, and interesting in its associations, so that no kind of effect could be introduced too striking or too impressive to portray it; and among the various appearances of the elements, we naturally look to the grander phenomena of Nature, as according best with the character of such a scene." Turner has matched the stature of his subject with a sky of unsurpassed intensity. His shepherd is as resolutely rooted in the landscape as the stones themselves, and seems to view the scene almost with detachment. He is accorded far more dignity than the shepherd struck down by lightning in J.M.W. Turner's *Stonehenge*, or the one musing on his shadow in Constable's view.

Reproduced in colour

The Visitors of the Ashmolean Museum, Oxford

70 The Nine Maidens, Morvah, Penwith, looking towards Zennor

(c.1845–50?)
Watercolour and bodycolour
22.3 × 34.6
Signed *W. Turner, Oxford*

Prov: E.T. Leeds, by whom presented, 1955.

The stone circle known as the Nine Maidens stands a few miles from Land's End, in a part of Cornwall which has been described as "littered" with standing stones, earthworks and ruins (W. Matthews, *Young Person's Guide to Cornwall*, 2nd ed., 1948, p.286). The pale yellow gleam on the horizon suggests a stormy evening; in the twilight, the stones, to the left, become virtually indistinguishable from the larger haystacks in the foreground. The merging of past and present thus finds yet another formal expression in Turner's art.

The scattering of brilliantly coloured strokes of bodycolour as finishing touches on a drawing executed in watercolour is a common characteristic of Turner's work in the 1840s and 1850s. The technique gives a surface sparkle, particularly valuable in large exhibition pieces, while often helping to give cohesion to the composition.

The Visitors of the Ashmolean Museum, Oxford

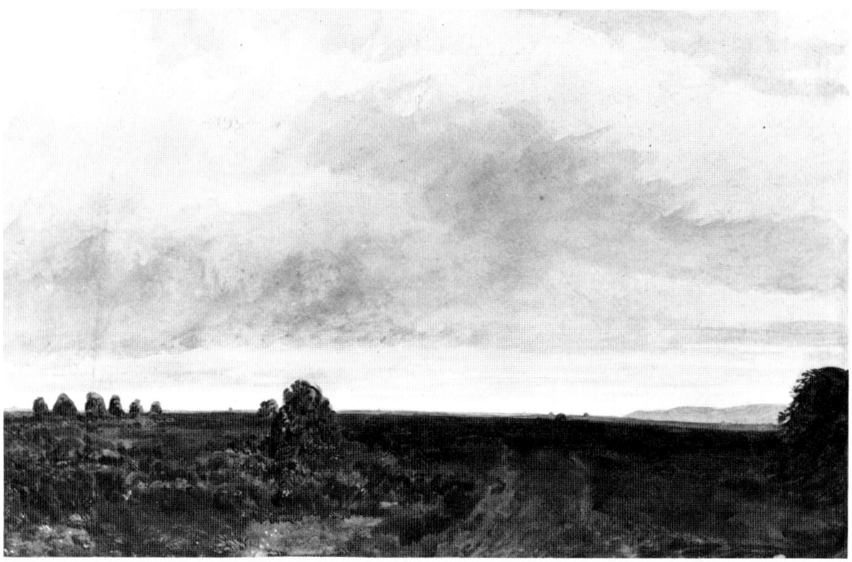

71 Roman Road near Dorchester

(c.1845–50?)
Watercolour with bodycolour on buff paper
16.5 × 26.7
Signed *Wm Turner* and inscribed *Study from nature in Dorchester field Oxon*

Prov: F.P. Morrell; Knight, Frank and Rutley, Black Hall, Oxford, 28 April 1925, lot 150 (part); bought Mrs Warren, 9½ guineas; by descent.

As one who spent much of his life travelling round the Oxfordshire countryside, Turner had an obvious personal interest in roads. Apart from the turnpikes with their all-too-frequent toll-bars, all the country villages were connected by a network

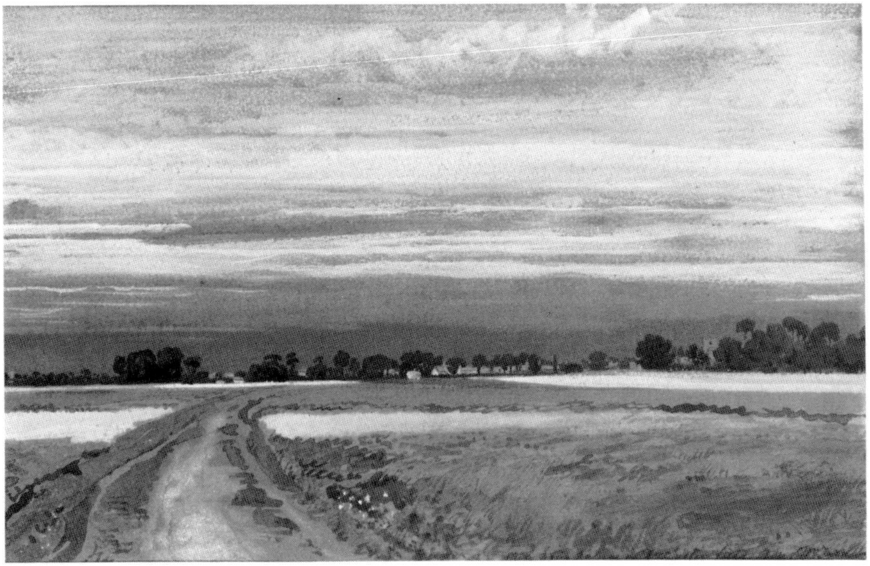

of tracks like the one depicted here until well into the nineteenth century. There is a latent irony in the comparison between the present muddy path and the power of the Empire this road once represented. Several studies in and around Dorchester exist, and it may well have been the historic associations of a town known to the earliest settlers, even before its Roman and Saxon prominence, which attracted Turner, although this is never made explicit. Another study, also depicting a track through a cornfield, and inscribed *Painted from Nature in Dorchester Field, Oxfordshire, Warborough, Benson & Ewelme in the distance* (Sotheby's, 18 March 1984, lot 11) in fact looks away from Dorchester towards the site of a British hill-fort, providing the eye with a sense of purpose as it ranges through the distance.

Private Collection

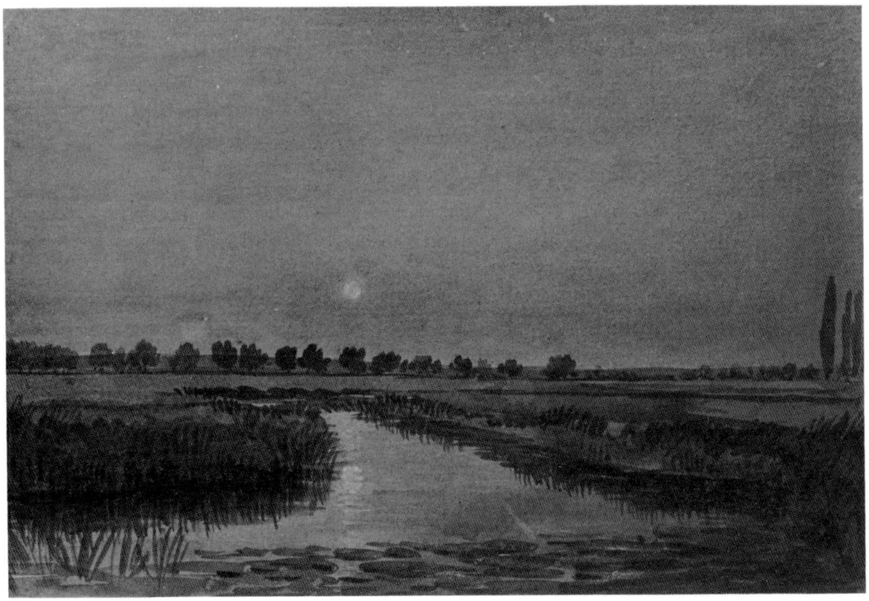

72 Full moon over the Cherwell

(c.1845–50?)
Watercolour with some gum, and bodycolour
24.2 × 34.9

Prov: Horatio Symonds, 1895.
Exh: UG(85), *Moonlight Scene near Oxford.*

Most of Turner's paintings of the Cherwell around Shipton portray the profusion of vegetation on its banks, which appears to close it off from any outside world. Here, by way of contrast, he has moved away to the open water-meadows, seen under a clear moonlit sky.

The very thin washes, with the darker greens having a slightly glazed quality suggesting the addition of very dilute gum, are most prevalent in studies of the 1840s. Many of the known moonlight and sunset studies also date from around these years.

Private Collection

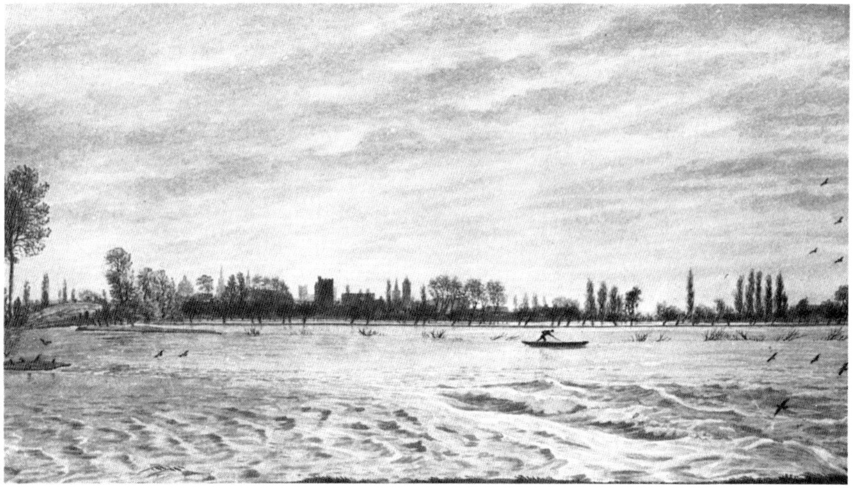

73 Portmeadow under flood: sunset

1847?
Watercolour
21 × 36.8

Prov: Studio sale, lot 143, £2.5s.6d. to Wyatt; Horatio Symonds, 1895.
Exh: ?SPW 1847 (181) *The Floods on the Meadows, near Oxford*, £15; Oxford Agricultural Show, 1878; UG (81).
Ref: *Saturday Review*, 31 August 1878.

This painting was associated in the catalogue of the 1895 exhibition with a work first exhibited in 1847, perhaps on the basis of information from the owner. Generally, a work priced at £15 would have been larger in size, but the exceptional detail here may have justified it. The painting is identifiable from a description in the *Saturday Review* as one shown among the "excellent little collection of pictures" by Turner at the Oxford Agricultural Show of 1878, where it is singled out for special praise: though the floods may be a "dreary and sombre" subject, the work "shows with what power and feeling Turner seized and expressed their melancholy sentiment".

Private Collection

74 Foliage study

(c.1845–55?)
Watercolour and bodycolour
27.2 × 46.7

During the 1840s and 1850s, Turner exhibited several works with the note, *Study from Nature* (see for example

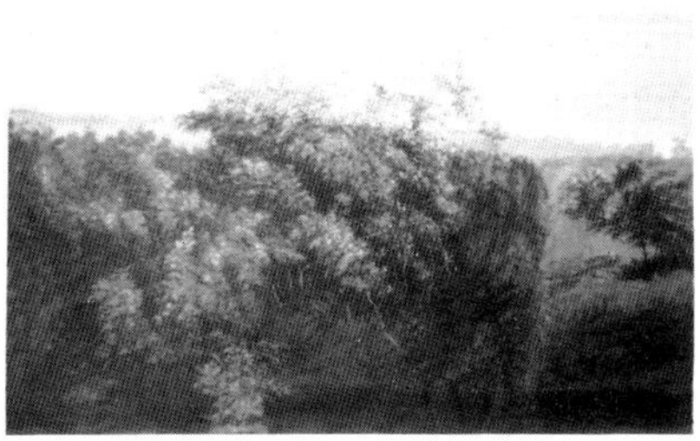

Cat.79), including, in 1855, a study of a hedgerow. This study of foliage is probably related to such works although nothing directly comparable has as yet come to light. In character it is quite close to Cat.72, particularly in the treatment of the distance. With Cat.79, these works may represent the range of a sketching style practised during the last two decades of his life. It is not possible to say whether they were actually finished in front of the subject, in true Pre-Raphaelite fashion; they do however show Turner focusing his attention on a specific corner of nature, in contrast to the more ambitious synthetic constructions he so often exhibited.

Private Collection

75 Cherwell Water-Lilies

1849
Watercolour and bodycolour
57.1 × 70.1

Prov: Given by the artist's executors, 1862.
Exh: SPW 1849 (218).

The decision of the Watercolour Society to form a Diploma Collection of members' works, corresponding to that of the Royal Academy, was made at a Council Meeting in December 1860, and the new law was implemented in 1861. Turner never in fact supplied a work, and this painting was donated to the Society by his executors.

Paintings of the River Cherwell were among Turner's earliest exhibited works. His early interest in the quiet stretches of the river spread with water-lilies, a subject literally on the doorstep of his uncle's manor at Shipton, may well owe something to his teacher Delamotte. Two very impressive oil-on-panel studies by Delamotte of the Isis at Waterperry, inscribed and dated 1805 and 1806, in the Yale Center for British Art, are certainly very close in character to the later works of Turner (see L. Hawes, *Presences of Nature, British Landscape 1780–1830*, Yale Center for British Art, 1982, Cat. IV.16 and IV.17).

Of the several known versions of *Cherwell Water-Lilies*, produced between the late 1830s and the 1850s, this is the only one that is dated.

The Trustees of the Royal Society of Painters in Watercolours, London

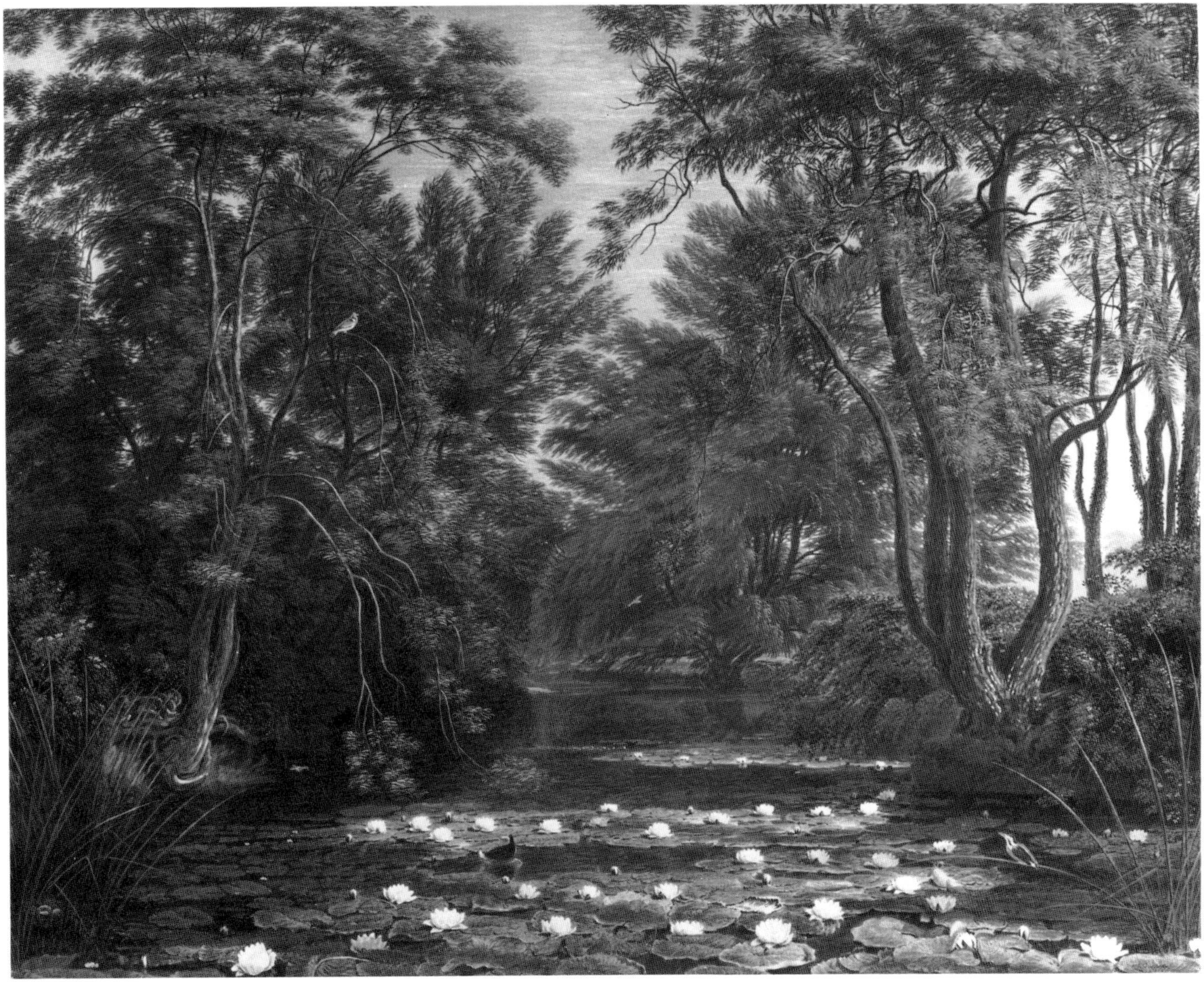

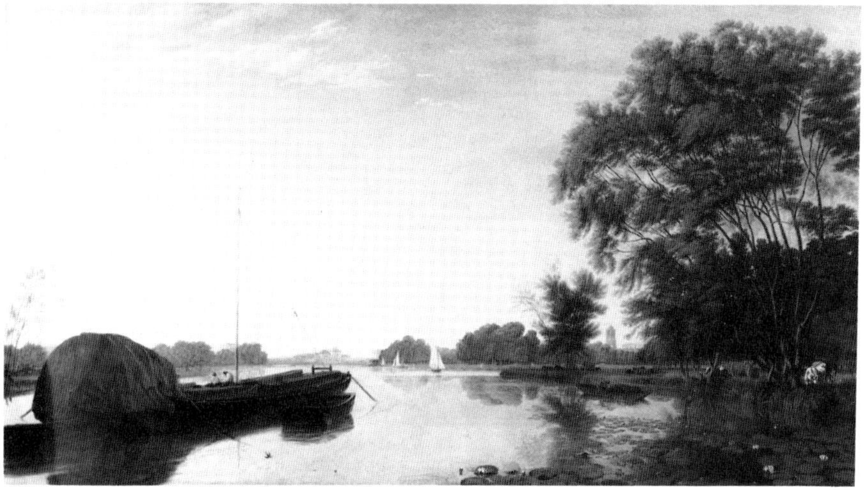

76 Oxford from the towpath

(c.1850?)
Oil on canvas
66 × 116

Prov: Rev. R.H. Lightfoot, by whom bequeathed 1954.

Topographical detail is kept to an absolute minimum in this view, only a glimpse of Tom Tower between the trees serving to identify the locality.

Throughout his career, Turner produced large-scale oil paintings. Most are variants of subjects also treated in watercolour, but he never seems to have been happy with oils. The majority of the works exhibited during the years when the Watercolour Society also hung oils (1813–20) he later destroyed. The few large oils that are known are invariably stiff and heavy, as if Turner felt obliged in such more pretentious work to present himself at his most impeccably formal.

If this oil of the River Thames achieves a degree of success, it is by preserving some of the delicacy of his handling of watercolour, rather than by any intrinsic merits. A very similar view, in watercolour, entitled *A Scene near the Junction of the River Isis and Cherwell – Evening* was exhibited in 1850 (SPW (50); Phillips, 24 November 1980, lot 144, repr.), and this oil is probably of similar date.

The Provost and Fellows of Worcester College, Oxford

77 View looking over Cowley Marsh from Bullingdon Green, near Oxford

1851
Watercolour and bodycolour
40.1 × 69.9

Prov: Sotheby's, 19 March 1970, bought Leggatt. Exh: SPW 1851 (179).

This is probably the painting exhibited in 1851; stylistically, it shows little variation from the *Portsmouth Harbour* of ten years earlier.

Turner relegates the city of Oxford to a thin wedge at the right-hand side of the picture, to concentrate on the flat and conventionally unattractive feature of Cowley Marsh. In a landscape

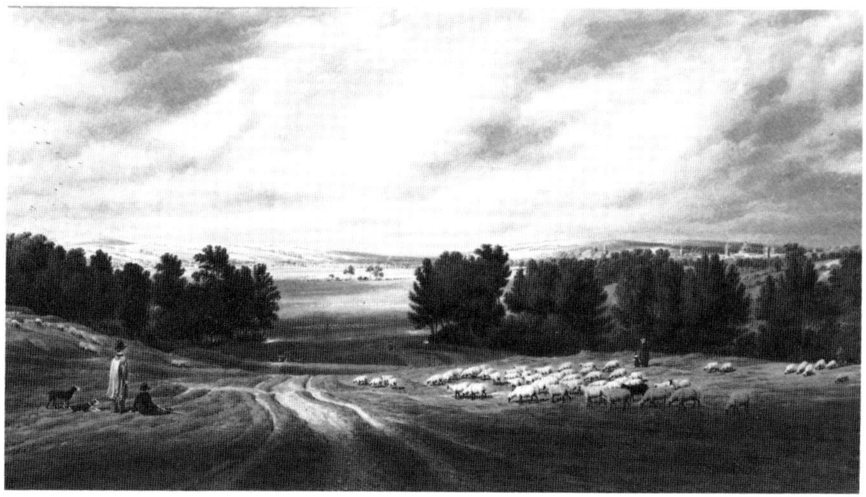

lacking any of the normal devices to lead the eye into depth, it is the six flocks of sheep which articulate the broad open space, and give a sense of scale to the distance. The overcrowded coach, careering along the London road towards Oxford, introduces a rare moment of genre, in counterpoint to the statuesque appearance of the shepherds.

Private Collection

78 View from the side of Bow Hill, on the South Downs, near Chichester, looking over the Groves of Yew Trees, and Stoke Park, towards the sea

1852
Watercolour, bodycolour and gum on cartridge
30 × 75
Signed *Wm Turner Oxford*

Prov: Professor Goldwin Smith, by whom presented.
Exh: SPW 1852 (197), £20, sold Prof. Smith; UG(145).

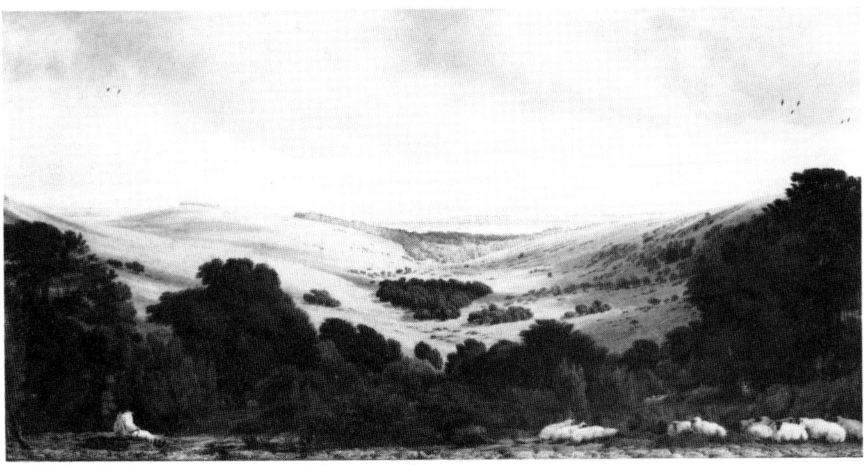

The contrast in mood with the earlier view (Cat.68) is extreme; signs of human activity are here suppressed in favour of a nature self-possessed, teeming with secret life.
The Master and Fellows of University College, Oxford

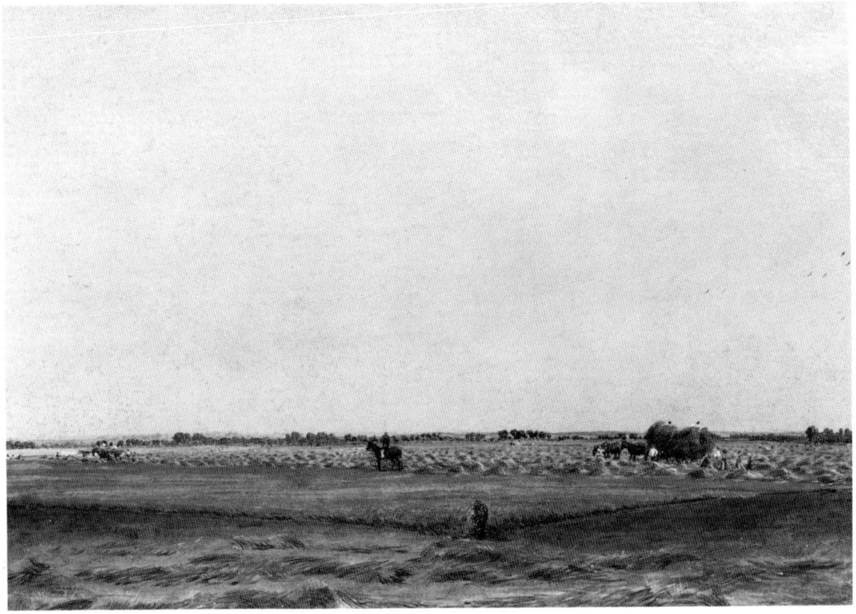

79 Haymaking – A Study from Nature, in Osney Meadow, near Oxford, looking towards Iffley

1854
Watercolour and bodycolour
25.4 × 35.6

Prov: F.P. Morrell; Knight, Frank and Rutley, Black Hall, Oxford, 28 April 1925, lot 169, bought Mrs Warren, 4 guineas; A.P. Warren sale, Sotheby's, 24 June 1971, lot 69, bought Agnew's.
Exh: SPW 1854 (78).

A late treatment of a subject recurring throughout Turner's career. He seems never to have tired of the varied formal options offered by the hayfield, imposing here the minimum of organisation on what is made to appear an almost unbounded space.

R.E. Alton, MC

80 Autumn – A View looking over Newell Plain, in Wychwood Forest, a spot well known in that part of the County to the frequenters of the Forest Fair

1854
Watercolour and bodycolour on cartridge
49 × 63
Signed *W. Turner Oxford.* Signed and inscribed on reverse *N° 3. Newell Plain in Wychwood Forest, Oxfordshire. W. Turner, Oxford*

Prov: Studio sale, lot 131, £4.15s.0d to Newman; Meatyard; purchased 1922.
Exh: SPW 1854 (174).

This view of Newhall Plain, as it is now called, in the heart of Wychwood Forest, has changed very little to this day. Only the foreground platform diverges from topographical accuracy. The ponds are the same as those appearing on the right of the early view (Cat.14), here seen from the South, as opposed to the North.

The choice of season, Autumn, and the prominent cleanly-sawn tree stump in the right foreground draw attention, in a combination of poetry and stark realism, to the imminent fate of the forest. An Act for the disafforestation of Wychwood was laid before Parliament in 1853, and though not passed until 1857, the first trees were sawn down in October 1856, and by 1858 thousands of acres of the ancient landscape had been cleared. The area seen here survived, but to Turner the whole forest, laden with associations personal and artistic, was under threat. Although Newhall Plain itself had been cleared long before, and become one of the features of the forest, its pale void provokes comparison with the wooded parts, sheltering a variety of wild and domestic fauna, so apparently on the brink of being reduced to the same slimy uniformity.

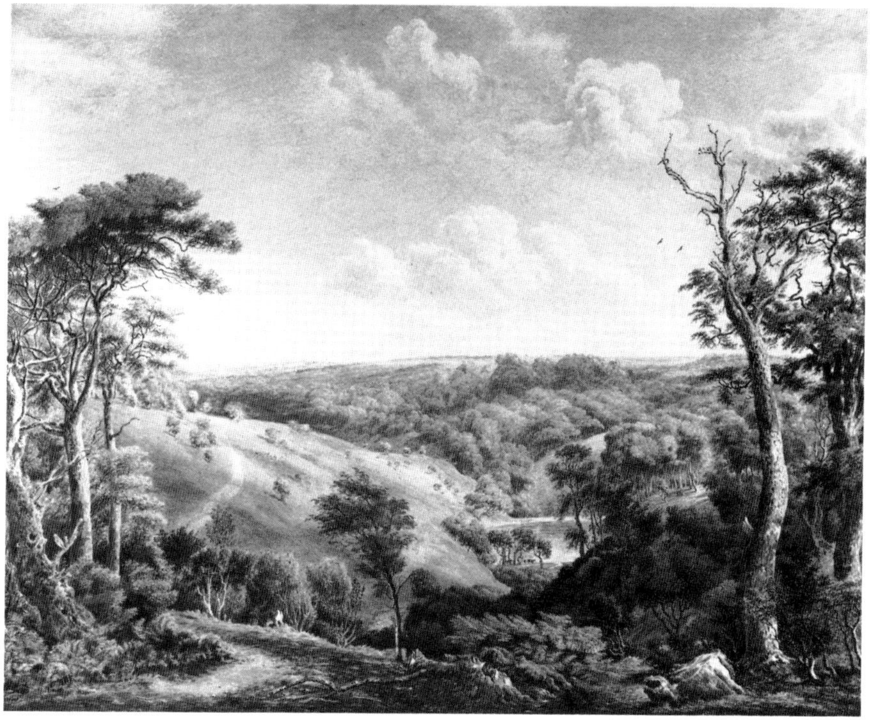

The Williamson Art Gallery and Museum, Birkenhead

81 Loch Coruisk

1855?
Watercolour and bodycolour
53.7 × 69.1

Prov: Rev. R. St J. Tyrwhitt; by descent; presented to Oxford City Council from the estate of B.E. Tyrwhitt.
Exh: ?SPW 1855 (62), *sold*; UG (92).

Possibly the watercolour exhibited in 1855 with a line from Scott's *Lord of the Isles*: "The evening mists with ceaseless change, etc." (Canto III, XV). In the hands of many of Turner's contemporaries, the proverbial darkness of the mountains serves as little more than a foil to the intrepid human presence, as for example in Robson's *Loch Coruisk*, introducing in the foreground Robert the Bruce, the hero of Scott's poem (repr. Hardie, pl.215). Here, there is no human presence to mediate for the viewer; the solitary eagle, as was remarked in another context, serves rather to "increase than diminish the wildness and desolation of the scene", (R. Chambers, *Picture of Scotland*, vol.2, 2nd ed., 1828, p.403). The spectacular "effect" in this work is entirely equal to the exceptional landscape, but in avoiding obscurity, and showing more of the form of the barren walls of rock manages to suggest a personal response.

Oxford City Council

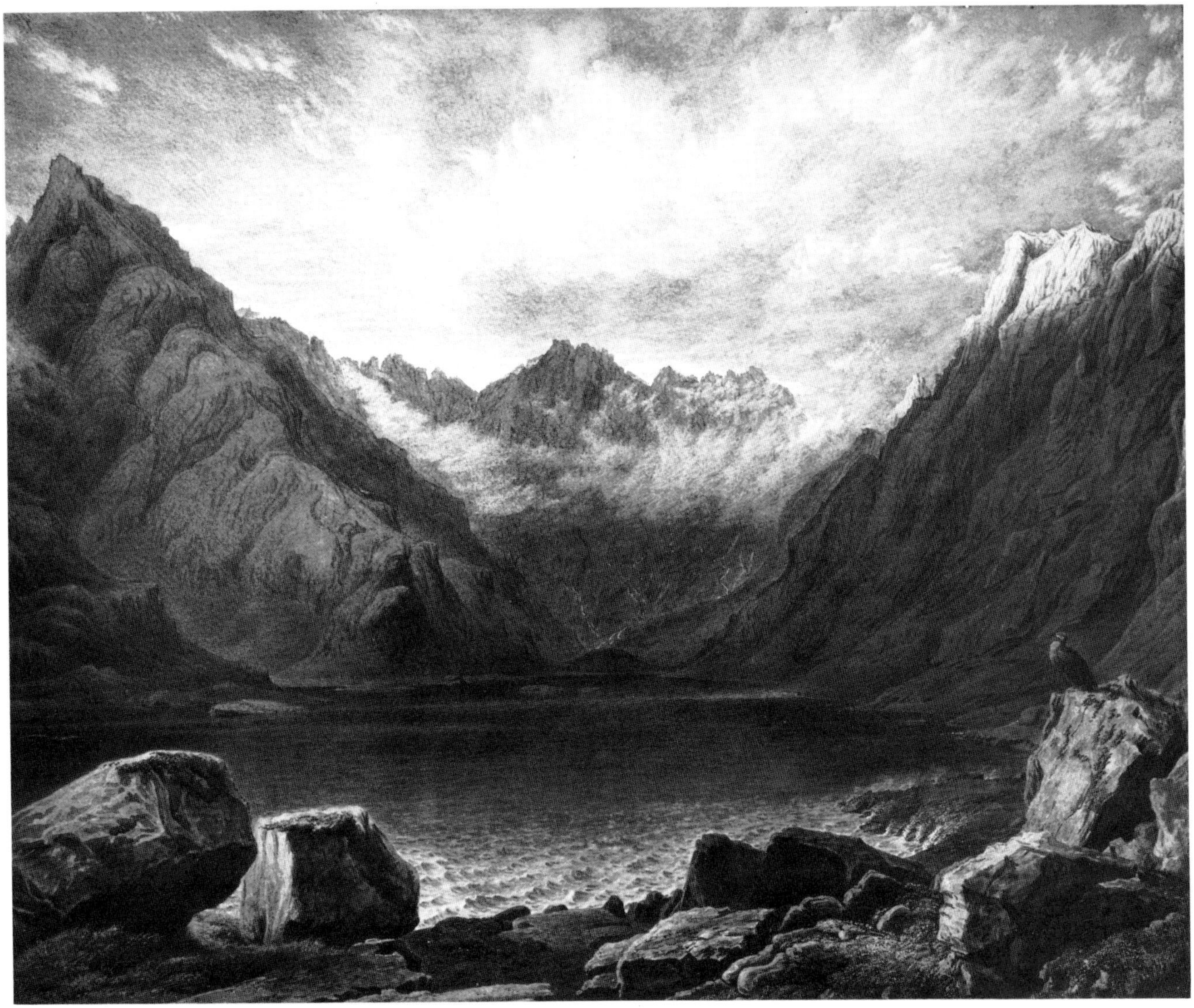

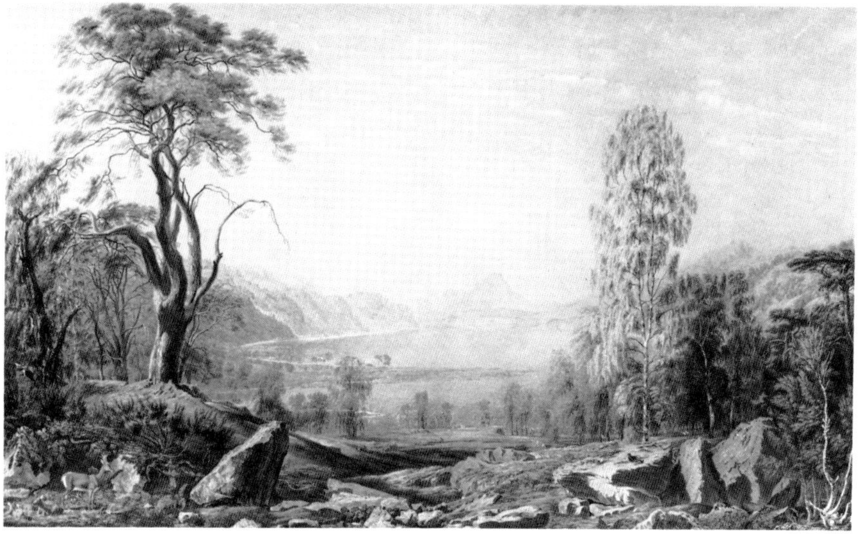

82 Loch Garry, Inverness-shire – Autumn

1856
Watercolour and bodycolour with scraping out
59.7 × 99.7
Signed *W. Turner / Oxford.* Inscribed on reverse *No.1 Loch Garry, Inverness-shire. N.B. Autumn*

Prov: Fine Art Society: Paul Thomas; Lawrence of Crewkerne, 18 December 1980, lot 3.
Exh: SPW 1856 (1), £40.

In August 1855 Turner was awarded the Watercolour Society's annual premium of 30 guineas in order to produce a large work for the following year's exhibition, and this is the result, the only securely documented example of a "Premium picture" of his career. He seems to have taken the unusual step of sending two contrasting works (the other was *Before Sunrise, Loch Torridon, Ross-shire*, untraced), but at £40 *Loch Garry* was the more highly valued; one of the highest prices he ever asked, it was that year equal to those of his more esteemed colleagues.

Loch Garry hardly merited a comment from most of the guide-books, a fact which may have endeared it to Turner. It is transformed here by the pale gleam of the invading pink light into a magical realm of stillness, where deer and grouse stand sentry, undisturbed and unthreatened by any human presence.

Mr Andrew Kimpton

83 A cock pheasant

1856
Watercolour and bodycolour on blue paper
15.8 × 34.5
Signed *W.T.* and inscribed *Jan.y 28 1856*

Prov: Agnew's, 1978.

Even at the end of his career, Turner did not cease to add to his stock of studies which might serve in large-scale works. The intense blue paper he often worked on lends a special depth of tone even to such seemingly casual sketches.

Private Collection

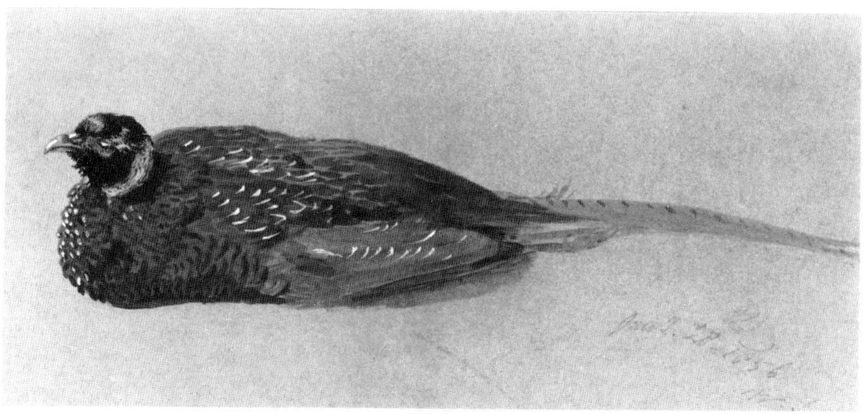

84 Kyleakin Castle, Isle of Skye

(c.1855–60?)
Watercolour and bodycolour
44.5 × 88.3

Prov: Ingram-Bywater Bequest, 1915.

During the 1840s and 1850s, Turner made a number of studies of sunsets vividly coloured in pinks, purples and orange. The combination in this finished work of evanescent lighting and isolated ruin produces a highly-charged blend of romanticism. The shimmering misty light which pervades the scene is a remarkable technical achievement in itself, yet produced with the simplest of means. The blue wash of the sky is worked all over with tiny dashes, some in a deeper tint of blue, others lighter, lifted out of the original wash with the tip of the wet brush.

The Visitors of the Ashmolean Museum, Oxford

85 Cherwell Water-Lilies

(c.1855–60?)
Watercolour and bodycolour
34 × 58.4
Signed and inscribed on back of old mount *Shipton on Cherwell. Wm. Turner*

Prov: Mrs Frederick Symonds; by descent to Miss Annie Symonds, by whom bequeathed, 1938.
Exh: UG (84).
Ref: Herrmann, p.245.

"A piece of close landscape, with water and pollarded willows, and the point of the subject is the effort of a young rustic to reach some waterlilies that grow in the water. The material is simple, but it's rendered interesting by the fidelity to nature by which it is characterised." This description refers not to Turner's picture, but to *The Water Lilies* by Walter Goodall (1830–1889), exhibited at the Watercolour Society in 1854 (*Art Journal*,

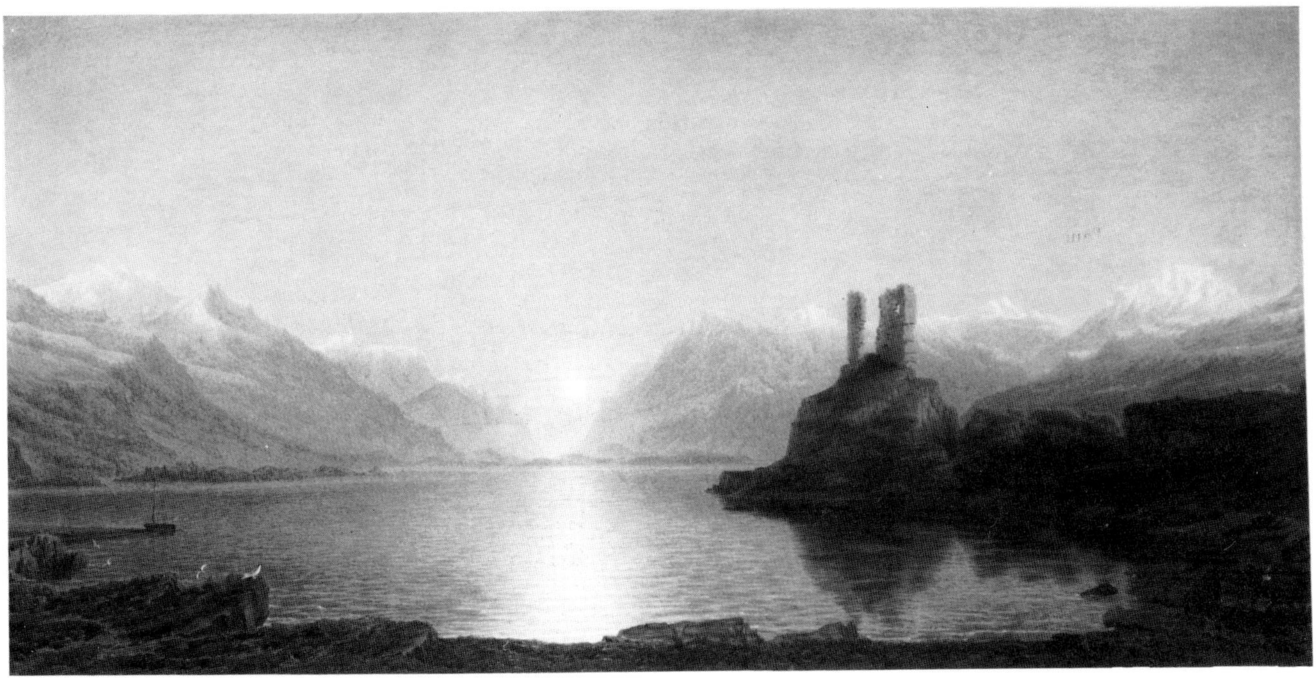

1854, p.174). It is interesting to find a contemporary of Turner's treating what has been viewed as an idiosyncratic subject in an apparently similar manner (close comparisons are impossible, as Goodall's work is lost). The quotation also draws attention to the total lack of "subject" in Turner's work, which dispenses even with the trivial activity which was seen to give "point" to Goodall's. Comparison with the other version of this subject exhibited here (Cat.74) reveals well the move towards unusual coloured lighting in the last decade of Turner's life. Although the last exhibited *Water-Lilies* appeared in 1851, this version probably dates from the second half of the 1850s; the addition of the tower of Shipton church on the extreme right acts as an added indication of the precise locality.

The Visitors of the Ashmolean Museum, Oxford

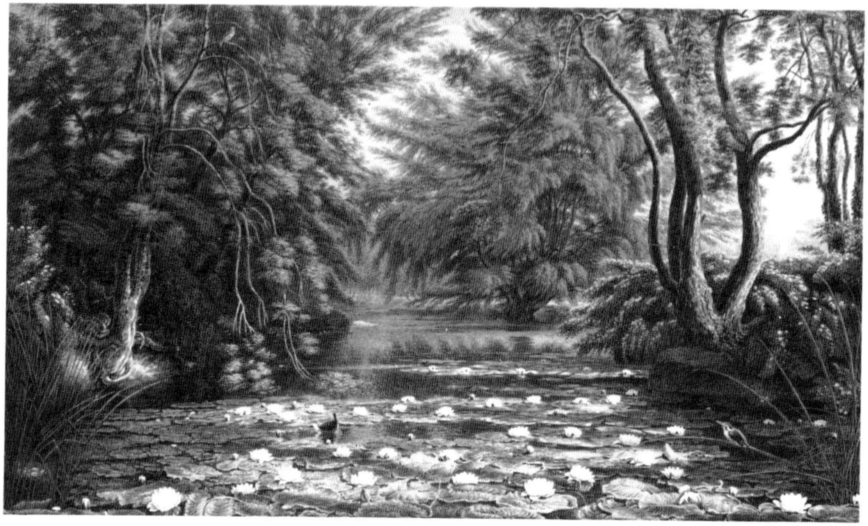

86 The Aurora Borealis

(c.1850–60?) 26.8 × 43.5

Black ink heightened with white on buff paper

Prov: Rev. R. St J. Tyrwhitt; by descent; presented to Oxford City Council from the estate of B.E. Tyrwhitt.

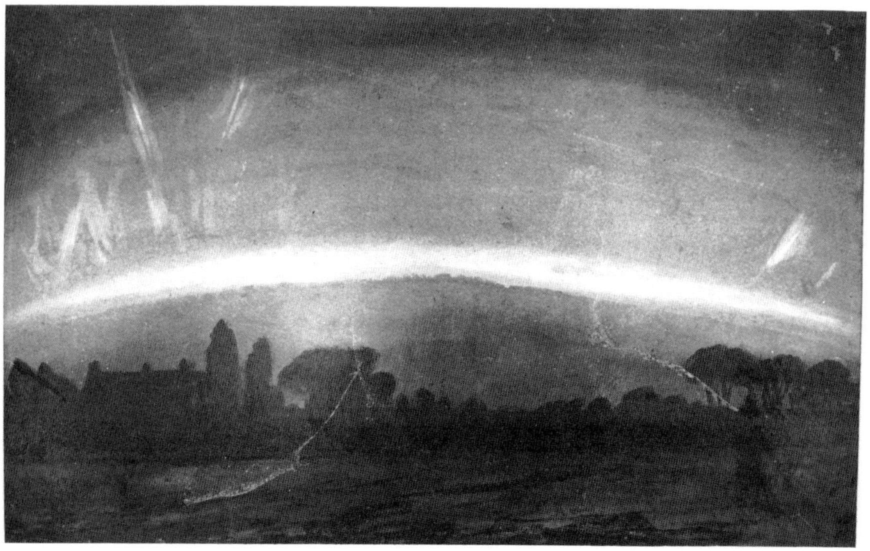

For Alison, most rapid movement was categorised as sublime, by virtue of its expression of power. In some instances, it could, however, be beautiful, and as examples he gives "the rapid shooting of the Aurora Borealis, the quick ascent of fire-works, a sudden stream of light from a small luminous object in the dark" (Alison, p.408).

For someone with as studied an interest in natural phenomena as Turner, it is only a small step from the observation of the day-time to the night-time sky. It is, nonetheless, surprising to find his two known excursions into astronomy so completely in tune with the Alisonian aesthetic, for if Alison mentions the Aurora by name, in the succeeding description he fully anticipates the depiction of the comet. It is left to Turner to illustrate the natural event Alison only intimates.

Oxford City Council

87 Donati's Comet

1858
Watercolour and bodycolour with some gum
25 × 36
Signed and dated *W. Turner / Oxford, 1858*

Prov: Sotheby's, 18 March 1982, lot 114.

This is a near replica of the work exhibited in 1859 with the title *Near Oxford – Half-past 7 o'clock P.M., Oct 5, 1858* (Mellon Center, Yale; see C. White, *English Landscape 1630–1850*, New Haven, 1977, no.194, repr. in colour).

Donati's comet was first observed in January 1858 over North America; during succeeding months it gained steadily in intensity, and could be seen all over Europe. On 5 October it attained its greatest brilliance. Even so, Turner's searing beam of light represents a response rather to the emotion than the visual reality of this climactic moment.

In the title Turner gave this work in the exhibition, he carried his propensity for exactitude to its extreme limit. The conjunction of that title with the image creates an effect far more profound than does the one used for convenience now. It causes the viewer to be aware not only of the vastness of space, and splendour of the universe which produces such spectacle; in identifying so precise, and so eminently transient a moment in time, Turner evokes every other individual moment, equally unique, equally transient, in an infinite succession.

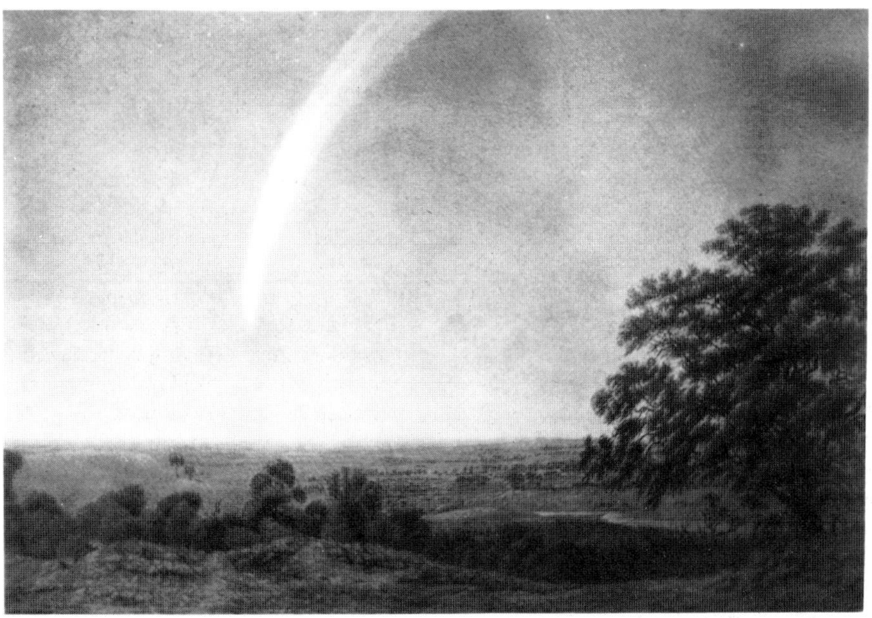

At least two other British artists painted pictures on the subject of the comet and both interpreted the event in a manner similar to Turner's. In William Dyce's *Pegwell Bay: A Recollection of October 5th 1858* (RA 1860, now Tate Gallery; see M. Pointon *The Representation of Time in Painting: A Study of William Dyce's Pegwell Bay . . . Art History* vol.1 no.1, March 1978, for a valuable analysis of this work) the comet is much less obviously visible in a day-time sky, but its role in fixing the scene to a particular temporal reality is still crucial. Along with Turner's watercolour in the exhibition of 1859 was another, by Samuel Palmer, entitled *The Comet of 1858 as seen from the skirts of Dartmoor*. Although generally a more overtly poetic artist than Turner, Palmer seems to have wanted to identify almost the same specific moment as both Turner and Dyce. In early October, the comet could be seen in conjunction with Arcturus. Palmer later explained to his friend Alexander Gilchrist, "I never had a proper title to my Comet drawing – for want of knowing on what day of the month I saw the thing represented – viz: the passing of Arcturus *through* the comet" (datable 20 May 1861; *The letters of Samuel Palmer*, ed. R. Lister, Oxford 1974, vol.II, p.603). Topicality in landscape painting was far from being an innovation for Turner; the widespread publicity attending such a sensational natural occurrence as the comet seems to have opened the eyes of other landscape painters to its imaginative potential.

Private Collection

Acknowledgments

While a considerable proportion of Turner of Oxford's work has remained in and around Oxford, much is now scattered, and our quest for this elusive personality has taken us to almost every county in England. In the course of our search we have incurred many debts, and it is a pleasure to be able to acknowledge them here.

Christopher Chasey's intuitive insight and passion for the artist have been a constant inspiration. He provided much valuable information, as did Elizabeth Jenkins and Marguerite and Robert Turner, all three descendants of Turner's uncle. Gabriel Naughton of Agnew's, James Miller and Henry Wemyss of Sotheby's and Edward King of Spink's have been unfailingly generous in helping to locate works and outstandingly patient in responding to a stream of enquiries. Special thanks are due to Michael Bryan and to Dr Christopher White of the Paul Mellon Centre for Studies in British Art, Michael Spender and Lynn Williams of the Royal Society of Painters in Watercolours, Roger Malbert of the Arts Council, Roy Stephens of the Marc Fitch Fund, Robin Griffith-Jones of Christie's, Peyton Skipwith of the Fine Art Society, Robert Mills of Sanders of Oxford, Andrew Wyld, Anthony Reed, Bill Thomson, John Barrows, Judith Chantry, Kathryn Park, Paul Atterbury, the Graves family, Michael Wilcox, Jane Cunningham, Gillian Saunders and Anne Buddle. Brian Mott of Oxford City Council, Dr Kenneth Garlick of the Ashmolean Museum and Dr Michael Kauffmann of the Victoria and Albert Museum and their respective staffs have responded willingly to heavy loan requests and many other demands, while Graham Brandon and Sally Chappell have taken much painstaking care over the photography.

During the course of our research, we have met many of the present owners of Turner's works. All have offered great encouragement, and their enthusiasm and generosity have been much appreciated. The many pleasurable memories of our visits are tinged with regret that the scale of the exhibition did not permit the inclusion of many more of the marvellous pictures we saw.

Many members of the County Museum staff have become involved in the project, offering their expertise and practical support. We should like to thank Eric Ogden, Kath Strange, Pat Crutch, Joy Pomfret, Philip Miles, Rodney James, Anne Phipps, Clarissa Pigott, Carol Nightingale, Carol Anderson, Sharon McDonald, Menaka Vachet-Beeston, Wendy Hillman, Joan Brasnett, David Eddershaw, David Smith, David Cross, Christopher Blake, Sheila Lambourne, John Steane, Ival Hornbrook, James Bond and above all Peter Gregory, Andrew Kitchen, John Rhodes, James Bateman and Judith Barrows.

It remains to thank the many friends and relations who have lived through this project; as Turner emerges from *eminence grise* into the glare of the spot-light, we are sure they will agree it was worth it.

Susie O'Reilly
Christopher Titterington
Timothy Wilcox

Photographic Acknowledgments

Thos. Agnew and Sons Limited; The Albany Gallery; The Ashmolean Museum, Oxford; Philip de Baye; The Bodleian Library, Oxford; Graham Brandon; The British Museum; Michael Bryan; Sally Chappell; Christie's; Courtauld Institute Photographic Survey; Prudence Cuming AssociatIon Limited; Michael Danny; The Grasmere Wordsworth Museum; Michael Dudley; The Fitzwilliam Museum, Cambridge; Colin Jeffrey Associates; P.J. Gates Limited; Martyn Gregory; Huntington Library, San Marino, California; Lawrence of Crewkerne; Leggatt Bros; City of Manchester Art Gallery; National Gallery of Scotland, Edinburgh; Newbery; Oldham Art Gallery; Reading Museum and Art Gallery; The Trustees of the Royal Society of Painters in Watercolours; Tom Scott; Sotheby's; Christopher Titterington; Victoria and Albert Museum; The Whitworth Art Gallery, Manchester; The Williamson Art Gallery and Museum, Birkenhead; The Witt Library, Courtauld Institute, London